# BACK AZIMUTHS

# BACK AZIMUTHS

## IT'S ALL ABOUT ... SHIPS

### Francis B. Burns

Deeds Publishing | Athens

Copyright © 2022 — Francis B. Burns

**ALL RIGHTS RESERVED**—No part of this book may be reproduced in any form or by any electronic or mechanical means, including information storage and retrieval systems, without permission in writing from the authors, except by a reviewer who may quote brief passages in a review.

Published by Deeds Publishing in Athens, GA
www.deedspublishing.com

Printed in The United States of America

Cover design by Mark Babcock.

ISBN 978-1-950794-75-1

Books are available in quantity for promotional or premium use. For information, email info@deedspublishing.com.

First Edition, 2022

10 9 8 7 6 5 4 3 2 1

*To my wife, Darlene:*
*You are my north, my south, my east, my west…*

# Advance Praise for Back Azimuths

"Colonel Francis Burns inspires as he takes us on a nautical tour of character building and leader development. *Back Azimuths* is a thought-provoking guide for leaders at all levels and a superb reference for personal, professional, and spiritual growth. Up anchor and immerse yourself in this rewarding Faith-filled journey provided by an exemplary Army Infantryman!"
—Saverio Manago, Associate Dean, Salem State University

"An insightful and inspiring book about…ships—written not by a Navy guy, but by an Army guy. The title is perfect. The author gives the reader an opportunity to reflect on their own life through his story, leading the reader on an emotional roller coaster throughout each…ship that comprises the book. I could not put it down. I loved this book."
—Chip Chase, Veteran

"Frank Burns is an exceptional writer. *Back Azimuths* is infused with life-long experiences, insights, and wisdom from a servant leader and educator. This highly-motivating book is written in a style that simply resonates. Clear and engaging, it is a must read for anyone desiring to explore their higher purpose."
—Colonel Roger L. Shuck, US Army, Retired

"*Back Azimuths* is an incredibly timely set of life instructions that we all need in today's chaotic world. Colonel Burns packages this self-help manual in a unique way that categorizes and creates balance in our human and spiritual lives. Reviewing our past efforts is something we all say we need to do, but often fail in every facet of true reflection. *Back Azimuths* will help us stay on our True Azimuth!"
—Colonel Edward (Ed) J. Reinfurt, US Army, Retired

"Colonel Frank Burns is full of SHIPs! *Back Azimuths* echoes memories of the foundational lessons instilled in us through our parochial education, expanding our minds, opening our hearts, and forging respect for those wonderful teachers and mentors who generously shared their tremendous talent and timeless wisdom. From our common background of growing up in a large Catholic family, marching along our parallel paths in the military, and wandering down diverging geographic paths, Frank shares his own valuable wisdom gathered through his 'ships' over the last half century. He articulates anecdotes, practical lessons, and insights for helping each of us to keep our moral compass straight as we navigate through an ever-changing world. With classical references and his sharp wit, he also reminds us of the importance of his "Five F's: Faith, Flag, Family, Friends and Fun." During the hectic pace of our daily lives, we can easily become distracted and roam off our best straight and narrow path in life. The insights provided in *Back Azimuths* help each of us to shoot our own back azimuth, returning us to our last known point in order to set out again upon the upright and moral path. Each of us should travel by…ship!"

— Patrick Donnelly, CFP, CPFA

"COL Francis Burns has written a brilliant book in *Back Azimuths*. Burns masterfully chronicles and reflects on his experiences at multiple echelons in the Army, coupled with his cogent approach to…ships. *Back Azimuths* is rife with timeless biblical quotes, stoic proverbs, and leadership examples woven together thru the author's masterful use of prose. Simply put, *Back Azimuths* should be recommended reading for all leaders who want to connect their faith to their personal development and growth along whatever career path or leadership journey they embark."

— COL Matthew T. Work, US Army

"This book is full of valuable lessons that would benefit military leaders. In an interesting memoir, the author's reflections tie insights from Christian tradition to experiences in a long and successful career as a leader. Reading *Back Azimuths* was like sitting with a respected military mentor who shares his wisdom on 21 different topics."

—Tim Grammel, Colonel, US Army, Retired, Former Military Judge

"*Back Azimuths* is what I needed to get back on track with my morning devotional time. The simplistic and concise format, coupled with the practical application and life lessons, make this a truly reflective and interactional masterpiece. In a world constantly filled with distractions, this book helps to illuminate the gift of slowing down and reflecting on what matters most."

—Chad Jenkins, 'Christ Over Fear' Host, YouTube | Jenkins Group LLC | Former FBI Agent & Army Ranger | Love Discussing Jesus, Leadership & Life

# Contents

| | |
|---|---|
| Foreword | xi |
| Ownership | 1 |
| Partnership | 9 |
| Friendship | 21 |
| Leadership | 31 |
| Marksmanship | 43 |
| Followership | 53 |
| Ambassadorship | 63 |
| Fellowship | 77 |
| Sponsorship | 91 |
| Mentorship | 97 |
| Scholarship | 109 |
| Stewardship | 117 |
| Worship | 129 |
| Workmanship | 137 |
| Membership | 147 |
| Sportsmanship | 159 |
| Hardship | 169 |
| Citizenship | 177 |
| Discipleship | 191 |
| Craftsmanship | 201 |
| Relationships | 213 |
| Conclusion | 227 |
| Acknowledgements | 229 |
| | |
| About the Author | 233 |

# Foreword

Just over ten years ago, I volunteered to go to Baghdad, Iraq for a one-year deployment. This was no small feat as I was a Permanent Professor and Department Head at the United States Air Force Academy with no real necessity to deploy. This presidential appointment, Senate confirmed position allowed me to remain at the Academy on active duty until the month before my 64th birthday educating the next generation of military officers. While it was comforting to know I was valued as an educator, the officership side of me necessitated that I volunteer. I had signed numerous deployment orders for others without any real hands-on experience in Iraq or Afghanistan. I knew it was my turn to serve alongside the women and men I had sent on deployment, and it was during this deployment that I met our author, Colonel Frank Burns.

Iraq in 2011 was a country attempting to become an independent nation-state yet unwilling to engage with the United States for a status of forces agreement. My memories include indiscriminate rockets, nightly alarms of "incoming, incoming, incoming;" attempts to reconcile irreconcilable demands from the Iraqis; trying to make sense of directives from our senior leaders, and stay sane working twenty hours a day, seven days a week, for months on end. Into this environment stepped Colonel Frank Burns, an Army Officer committed to making rational recommendations to our superiors, despite the irrationality of our daily meetings and trips in up armored vehicles and daily flights in Blackhawk helicopters. He cared deeply about all our mission challenges, including how to survive this deployment without a status of forces agreement, how to convince contractors to stay in this tumultuous environment with no legitimate guarantees for their safety, and how to keep the troops motivated to complete ambiguous and ill-defined missions. These were tough times, and yet the right leadership combination made sure we brought everyone safely home from that initial cadre of troops.

Frank was an integral part of that leadership team, and he made every day sane and worthwhile for his peers and subordinates, thanks to his insights, experiences, and education. We attended weekly mass together and kept our faith strong during these trying times. Frank assisted me through many tough days, and we found a common faith and commitment to our Constitution that led to numerous conversations over those months. I know I would not have survived as well without Frank Burns. He honored me by mentioning me in his mentorship chapter; the truth is…Frank inspired us all with his faith, experiences, leadership, and his sense of humor.

Even a decade after our deployment, Frank Burns is one of those individuals I know I could turn to, and he would give me the shirt off his back and ask what else do you need. He is one of those leaders who I would serve with and for anywhere, anytime, at any moment.

This book is a culmination of his life experiences and perspectives. He explores memories that are etched into our consciousness, especially for those of us who were in the Pentagon on September 11, 2001. He challenges his readers to think about our purpose, our values, and our perspectives in every aspect of our lives. Our author draws you in with his play on words. Why in the world would an Army Officer care about ships? Is that not the purview of the Navy? He defines "ships" and each chapter is a collection of thoughts and ideas around a particular "ship" such as citizenship, friendship, and leadership. His framework for analysis includes insights, inspirations, and reflection questions. He has gathered a lifetime of ideas, thoughts, quotes, and perspectives from which we can benefit.

Time is one of our most valuable commodities in today's fast-paced society with instantaneous communications. This book challenges us to be a little more reflective and to slow down to think about what our lives are meant to be. "Living the Dash" is one of my favorite phrases and one that requires you to think about how you want to live your life. What do you want your legacy to be? This author articulates the five "F's"—faith, flag, family, friends, and fun. He reminds us that every individual is on a journey, and we can learn from one another by reading about others' journeys just as we read histories of great individuals.

Those who serve our nation in the military have the added benefit of experience—we live all over the world, we personally observe other cultures close up, and we find ways to interact and adapt with others who may not share our faith, our family values, or our moral foundations. We serve with them and for them to meet national security objectives set by our political leaders. In times of great political stress and turmoil, there is much that can be learned from these experiences and may assist us in turning down the volume and rhetoric of disillusionment facing our nation today.

Military veterans reflect lives of service—we stand on the shoulders of those who have served before us, and we can learn much from these individuals, whether they are our founding principles of this nation or just being a decent human being toward others with a willingness to listen to different perspectives without hateful conclusions. We serve our nation, our fundamental values, and a higher being—this book offers the opportunity for the reader to think deeply about purpose and guiding principles for their own lives. What is important to you? Do you care about sportsmanship? Does stewardship mean much to you? How about scholarship? What about life-long learning and the opportunity to grow intellectually and spiritually throughout your life?

For those whom faith means little, perhaps this book offers the opportunity to explore spirituality in a non-confrontational way as human beings are social creatures, and we have an opportunity to learn from the experiences of another individual who has spent his life in service to others—whether they are fellow veterans, fellow believers, or fellow citizens. This book challenges the reader to think deeply about life's challenges and ways in which we can grow in our faith, our commitment to our American values, and to one another as individuals. We can begin a dialogue with others using the tools outlined by the author. Every discussion about any of the ships could begin to heal relationships and give individuals the inspiration to think deeply about this journey called life.

At Arlington National Cemetery, several quotes are located around the various structures to reflect the honored, hallowed ground of those individuals who gave the ultimate full measure of their lives for this nation. One quote resonates with members of the military, active duty and veterans alike. Attributed to George Washington, the quote at the Arlington Memorial Amphitheater reads, "When we assumed the soldier, we did not lay aside the citizen." [1] I frequently used this quote to challenge my students to think deeply about their commitment to our Constitution and

---

1. Clint W. Ensign. Inscriptions of a Nation Collected Quotations from Washington Monuments; Washington D.C., Congressional Quarterly, 1994, pg. 112.

a realization that you are always a representative of the United States.

Colonel Frank Burns is one of the best examples of this duality and his reflections in this book will challenge his readers to look deeply into their own commitments to our nation. Further, in Washington D.C. there are numerous buildings that contain famous quotes from our most remarkable heroes. James Madison, one of our founding fathers and the architect of our Constitution once wrote, "Knowledge will forever govern ignorance: And a people who mean to be their own governors, must arm themselves with the power which knowledge gives." [2] This book adds knowledge, and this collection of ideas and perspectives will make you laugh and cry just as any good book should and I hope you enjoy the journey as much as I did.

—Dr. Cheryl A. Kearney, PhD
Brigadier General, United States Air Force, retired
Professor Emeritus, United States Air Force Academy

May 2022

---

2. Ensign, pg. 38.

*OK now, listen up. If you ever find yourself not knowing where you are, first, you need to get out your map, your protractor, and your compass. Then with your compass, shoot a good, straight back azimuth to your last known point.*
—Land Navigation Instructor, Fort Benning, GA, circa 1986 [3]

The simple words of a non-commissioned officer (or sergeant) who was in charge of our land navigation training at Fort Benning, Georgia in 1986 still itch at my ears. I am now beginning to understand how back azimuths and...ships are interrelated.

...ships. The actual root is from Old English *scipe*, meaning to shape. It denotes a state or condition, character, office, skill, etc. [4]

Originally, I wanted to write that everything I learned in the Army I learned from my time at the US Naval War College — it's all about...ships! Seriously though, by the addition of the suffix...ship to the end of certain words, the word then becomes something to which one should aspire. This book is not to be confused with the ships passage that was so elegantly written by Longfellow, about ships passing in the night. At least not on the surface.

This book will be divided by different...ships that have a certain meaning to me. Each chapter will begin with a definition of

---

3. Francis B. Burns. Personal Notes. Most of the notes are kept in 5"x 8" green notebooks, which are favored by military personnel to take notes, tasks, and organize their work.

4. The Compact Oxford English Dictionary, 2nd ed. Clarendon Press: Oxford, 1998. All definitions in this book use the Oxford Classical Compact Dictionary.

the…ship, which was taken from the Compact Oxford English Dictionary (one of the last dictionaries to be typeset). Then, using the words *Insight*, *Inspire*, and *Ignite*, I further detail thoughts on that specific…ship, as well as offer questions to contemplate related to that specific…ship.

**Insight:** I use a Bible verse that has significant meaning to me. Many have used similar verses or quotes in order to develop their moral compass, in fact, there may be several verses of significance, related to or unrelated to the specific…ship. I believe that it is important to have something of value on which to build a life of meaning.

**Inspire:** I would like to think that the greyer or even less hair on the temple, the more of a thinker one becomes, as there seems to be more time for proper reflection on what really matters. I have in turn used the Bible verse as an anchor, in a sort of educational experience way, as there are certainly lessons to be learned, unlearned, then re-learned.

**Ignite:** By properly understanding *Insight* and what *Inspires* us, I believe that this should in turn spark a certain emotive response and action in order to better ourselves.

In each chapter, I offer a collection of thoughts on the…ship, a connection of the meaning of the…ship to me, different talks and thoughts that I have given that emphasize the specific…ship. I end each chapter with some short reflections that I have taken from each…ship. Finally, each chapter concludes with some questions to the reader to reflect upon and to take action. This technique may stem from being in the audience and attempting to garner a message from a speaker or lecturer. It could also be a product of synthesizing weekly messages from homilies at a Catholic Mass, or another religious service.

During the Catholic Mass and following the Introductory Rites, the Liturgy of the Word, and prior to the Liturgy of the Eucharist, a Catholic priest or deacon delivers a homily. During the Liturgy of the Word, the *Insight* phase, the congregation listens to the readings from the Bible: First Reading (usually an Old Testament Verse), a Responsorial Psalm (from the Book of Psalms), a Second Reading (from the New Testament), and then a reading from one of the four Gospels (Matthew, Luke, John, or Mark), also from the New Testament. During the homily, I believe that the priest or deacon should then *Inspire* in us a connection into the proper context in which it was written. Then, as we contemplate on the message, it should *Ignite* in us a Judeo-Christian response to action.

It is not necessary to read the book sequentially. If there is a specific…ship that sparks your interest, or is near and dear to you, please delve into that chapter. The thoughts expressed in this book stem from years of taking notes, copying articles, absorbing quotes that have special meaning to me, and living out each…ship. So, it is part leadership manual, part lessons learned, part memoir. The examples of each…ship can be traced back to William Shakespeare's thoughts that "And 'tis a kind of good deed to say well; and yet words are not deeds,"[5] or as the US Army's 22nd Infantry Regiment motto reads, "Deeds Not Words." My hope is that the reader is able to respect, understand, and appreciate just how much each…ship is interrelated.

---

5. And 'tis a kind of good deed to say well: And yet words are no deeds. Shakespeare Quote. Retrieved December 20, 2021 from https://www.playshakespeare.com/henry-viii/scenes/act-iii-scene-2..

# Ownership

To make (a thing) one's own, appropriate take possession of.

**Insight:** Genesis 1:26.

*"Then God said: "Let us make man human beings in our image, after our likeness. Let them have dominion over the fish of the sea, the birds in the air, the tame animals, all the wild animals, and all the creatures that crawl on the earth."* [6]

With ownership comes responsibility. Since at least from 1982 when I enlisted in the Army, it has been emphasized that the two basic responsibilities of a non-commissioned officer are mission accomplishment and taking care of Soldiers. Recently, the Chief of Staff of the Army and the Sergeant Major of the Army have changed this mantra to People First, Mission Always, and made it applicable to all in the Army. This selflessness of caring for and taking responsibility of Soldiers is now forefront in word and deed.

**Inspire:** When I think of ownership, I think of the phrases such

---

6. Genesis 1:26. Catholic Study Bible, Oxford University Press. 2010. All Bible references in this book use The Catholic Study Bible.

as, "You bought it, you own it," or, "You signed for it, you own it," and, "Treat the equipment as if you own it, because you do." In 1987, I was a Lieutenant (the lowest officer rank) in Kirchgoens, in the then Federal Republic of Germany, inventorying four each M113 Armored Personnel Carriers (APCs) and all the accompanying equipment. These would be the tracked vehicles and equipment in which we would literally roll out of our kaserne and move to our local dispersal area, then to our planned defensive position, should the then Soviet Union decide to cross the West German border. As one increased in rank, the ownership, responsibility, and accountability level also increased.

**Ignite:** Leave things better than when you've found them.

*Fort Polk, Louisiana, January 2011. Groundbreaking Ceremony, Warriors In Transition Barracks. Pictured in photo are Brig Gen James C. Yarbrough, Command Sergeant Major Jeffrey Hof, Col. Kelly Murray, Command Sergeant Major Ted Sutton, Warrior In Transition Commander (Lieutenant Colonel) and Command Sergeant Major. That's me, on dirt mound, in white safety cowboy hat.*

I believe that caring for service members may stem from a promise from President Abraham Lincoln's second inaugural address in 1865: "To care for him who shall have borne the battle and for his widow, and his orphan."[7]

This is now the first part of the mission statement of Veterans Affairs, who "serve and honor the men and women who are America's Veterans.[8]

The below remarks were delivered in January 2011, while the Global War on Terrorism was ongoing. It was given while I was serving on Active Duty in the US Army, at Fort Polk, LA, for the Soldier Family and Assistance Center's (SFAC) Groundbreaking Ceremony.

*Good Afternoon!!*

*Welcome to today's ribbon cutting ceremony for the Soldier Family Assistance Center.*

*We have asked an awful lot of soldiers, especially our Wounded Warriors, now we are recognizing that where they conduct their everyday business is very important. As we talked about a few months ago with the groundbreaking of the Warriors in Transition Unit (WTU) Barracks, it is indeed the Soldiers themselves, through their blood, sweat, and tears, who have paid for every brick, nail, and square foot of concrete of this building.*

*This SFAC is part of the Warrior Transition Complex and will be completed in three phases. Phase I is the Soldier Family Assistance Center (SFAC), on which we are cutting the ribbon*

---

7. Veterans Affairs (VA), mission statement. Retrieved on December 20, 2021 from https://www.va.gov/about_va/mission.asp.

8. Ibid.

today. The Barracks are Phase II of the WTU complex. It will be 67,000 square feet, 112 Rooms at a cost of about $17M: translation = $152K each Soldier, or as Adam Sandler sings, "Not too shabby." Completion of the barracks is slated for 9 OCT 11 — Colonel Shuck, you will be here in my stead to cut the ribbon on that facility. Phase III will be the new headquarters complex, scheduled to be completed JAN 12. So, the Warriors in Transition (WT) Soldiers and Cadre will live, work, and be taken care of in one complex, with Baynes Jones Army Community Hospital (BJACH) and all that it offers to the WT Soldiers and their families right across the street. A Win-Win situation.

 The concept of a Soldier and Family Assistance Center began in 2003 at Fort Sam Houston's Brooke Army Medical Center where military doctors recognized a need for Family members' involvement in the recovery of their wounded Soldiers. Now, that fledgling program is permanent, with SFACs established across both large and small garrisons.

 Fort Polk has been providing Soldiers and their Families the assistance they need for several years at the Army Community Service Family Readiness Center. The program here is going to be strengthened and solidified with this new $4.6 million dollar facility that provides a network of Family services dedicated to the needs of our Warriors in Transition and their Families.

 The SFAC offers assistance, not only to Soldiers wounded in combat, but also those injured during training. The goal is to set Soldiers and Families up for success, whether those Families are going back into the mainstream of the Army or into the civilian sector.

 Services available at the SFAC include:

- *Entitlement and benefits counseling*
- *VA benefits and entitlements*
- *Legal assistance*
- *Pastoral services*
- *Transition and employment services*
- *Childcare and youth services*
- *Family Life consultants, substance abuse counseling and more.*

This building would not have occurred without input from the customers—folks at the US Army Medical Department Activity (MEDDAC)—and our Department of Public Works (or DPW) Team consisting of Ellis Smith, Scotty Goins, Lorna Hanes, and Shane Gremillion. Thank you for your tireless efforts in making this installation a better and more efficient place to work and live.

You deserve the best the Army has to offer—facilities and programs that are commensurate with the level of your service and sacrifice. This SFAC—and the remainder of the WTU complex to follow—is dedicated to the Soldiers and Families who will benefit from the services that will be provided. This is a great addition for the installation, the community and for the WT Soldiers.

*Army Strong.*
*Support and Defend.*
*All the Way.*
*Thank You.*

Francis B. Burns

## Personal Reflection

- Be it a piece of equipment or establishment of systems and standing operating procedures, the mantra that I try to follow is that we should always be creating, building, making things better than when we found them.
- It is remarkable the difference of the responsibility of 30 Soldiers and four vehicles in 1987, compared to the cost of the SFAC facility and the amount of folks who will utilize the WTU complex.

## Contemplate:

Describe the first item that you owned? How did that make you feel?

_____
_____
_____
_____
_____
_____

In what way have you displayed ownership in my life? At home? With your Family? At work?

_____
_____
_____
_____
_____
_____

How have you "paid it forward?" At home? With your Family? At Work?

_____
_____
_____
_____
_____
_____

# Partnership

Partaker, sharer, association, participation.

**Insight:** 1 Corinthians 13:4-8.

> *Love is patient, love is kind, love does not envy, love does not boast, love is not proud, love does not dishonor others, love is not self-seeking, love keeps no record of wrongs.*

What strikes me first from this verse is that love is not self-seeking, it is selfless. It can translate to the expression that no one is an island. Our lives are woven into others in ways we often do not understand. In the Christmas film, *It's a Wonderful Life,* starring Jimmy Stewart and Donna Reed, one of the biggest take-aways is that you do not know how much your life or example will impact others.[9]

**Inspire:** James Hunter, in a leadership session given in November 2020, given via MS Teams to the US Army Installation Management Command (IMCOM) Garrison Command Teams, noted

---
9. 52 Little Lessons from It's a Wonderful Life, Bob Welch. Thomas Nelson, Inc, 2021.

that 1 Corinthians 13:4-8 is perhaps one of the most quoted Bible verses.[10]

It was in fact a reading at our marriage ceremony at Fort Drum, NY in 1993. Many have been taught to substitute a name of someone who is dear to you in lieu of the word love.

With that, I offer my father-in-law's eulogy and graveside service reflection. My father-in-law, George S. Archie, Jr., died in January 2020. Although the funeral was held in early January, due to COVID-19 travel restrictions, we were unable to bury him in the Veterans Affairs Cemetery in Tampa, Florida until December 2020. Poppy did indeed emulate this verse in his life.

**Ignite:** Love

---

10. Burns Personal Notes.

# Back Azimuths

*To leave the world a bit better, whether by a healthy child, a garden patch, or a redeemed social condition; To know even one life has breathed easier because you have lived. This is to have succeeded.*

—*Ralph Waldo Emerson*

*Good morning. I am Francis B. Burns, Colonel, US Army (Retired), and have been the son-in-law of George Archie for the past 26 years.*

*Through his service in Korea and the linkage to my namesake, his acknowledgement of what his time in the United States Marine Corps did for him, and that I married his daughter, we had a special bond.*

*He served as a mentor and father figure to me. Although I served in the Army, my namesake is USMC Corporal Francis B. Burns, who served and died in the Korean War. I share his date of death as it is also my birthday, albeit 13 years later.*

*I mention the Korean War as Pop was fond of saying of his time in the Marine Corps, "I made Staff Sergeant in two years!" As you also know, he served in the Korean War as a Crew Chief on a then 'new' piece of equipment, the helicopter. Those were the days being up close and personal to Sikorsky engines all day, prior to ear protection. You can now appreciate that his hearing loss was due to the effects of the helicopters. He spent many blade hours in the village of Panmunjom, just north of the future Demilitarized Zone (DMZ), for the Korean Peace Talks. I believe that one his happiest moments in recent memory was when he visited us at the Naval War College in Newport, Rhode Island and met the current commander and pilots of his old helicopter unit from Korea, and sat with and among fellow Marines as we had a lecture on the Korean War.*

*He was indeed proud of his 'service,' a word that seems to be taken too lightly nowadays.*

*His glass was always half-full. Whenever you asked him how he was, he never complained. "I'm alright. Thank God."*

*He related well to all with whom he came in contact. He was able to use his Italian to speak broken Spanish when he worked.*

*He saw a silver lining in every experience. From Darlene starting medical school with a newborn son, to driving all of the kids around all night in the car, so Darlene could get some rest; Getting our house established during many Army moves; Saying it was a good experience for our first Au-Pair/ Nanny to have failed her driver's test several times — "At least she's learning from it."*

*Lastly, he taught me through example what it was like to be a caring husband, as he loved Peg beyond measure, as well as how to be a wonderful and great father, grandfather, and great-grandfather, who consistently exhibited wisdom and patience to no end.*

*In our tears, let us smile in that he is now with Peg, and so many other loved ones.*
*Grief is the price we pay for love.*

*In closing, I would like to offer a version of a poem, entitled, The Watch:*

*For eighty-eight years,*
*This Marine has stood the watch.*

*While some of us lay about our bunks at night,*
*This Marine stood the watch.*

## Back Azimuths

*While others of us were attending schools,*
*This Marine stood the watch.*

*And, yes, even before many of us were born,*
*This Marine stood the watch.*

*As our families watched the storm clouds of war brewing on the horizons of history,*
*He stood the watch.*

*This Marine looked ashore and saw his family often needing guidance,*
*but he knew that he must stay because he had the watch.*

*For eighty-eight years he stood the watch so that*
*Our fellow countrymen could sleep soundly, in safety,*
*Knowing that this Marine would stand the watch.*

*Today we are here to say,*
*The watch stands relieved.*

*Relieved by those you have led, guided, and trained.*
*Staff Sergeant Archie, you stand relieved.*

*We have the watch.* [11]

*Semper Fi. Love you Pop.*

---

11. The Watch, Retrieved December 1, 2020 from https://poets.org/poem/watch.

Francis B. Burns

## Graveside service, 11 months later.

*I am humbled to say a few words this afternoon.*

*1 Corinthians 13:4-8*

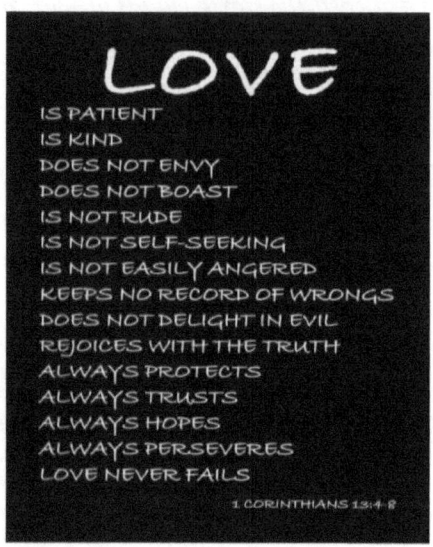

I know what you're thinking. This is a memorial service not a wedding, why are you reading this? Darlene is watching this via Facebook live and she's thinking, "Oh no. Does he have the COVID? The Rona?"

We should have known it was not going to be a good year as we started out the year by losing Pop, and close to the year's end are now placing him next to his soulmate, Peg. Wish we all could be here, together.

In 1 Corinthians Chapter 13, Paul explained how important love is in a person's life. He said that even though someone *has many gifts and things on this earth, without love they are somewhat useless.*

*We can have marvelous gifts used to help people and bring joy to those who need it, but without love, our works here on this earth will be useless.*

*Or, to use a country song reference: "Never seen a hearse with a trailer hitch."*

*Believe that our remembrance of Pop stems from the universal & timeless principle of love found in that Bible verse.*

*He was about Serving.*

*He was about putting love into action and that action is service.*

- *Service equals Love.*
- *It's an act of love, it's a verb.*
- *It's what you do.*
- *Love takes action.*
- *Love in action is service.*

*1 Corinthians 13:4-8. It's one of, if not the, most quoted Bible verses, and words of literature.*

*It's about Love/ Leadership/ Character/ Integrity-all which Pop possessed in abundance.*

*Allow me to go through some of the words, and let us pause, remember, and reflect on the example set by Poppy in word and deed.*

## Love is patient

*Patience is defined as Impulse Control. With that he taught his sons to trap and hunt, Darlene and I how to be good parents, and offered the gift of time and patience with his grandkids, great grandchild, and friends.*

## Love is kind

*Kindness is defined as: Gratitude; Encouragement; Candor; Appreciation, Courtesy. He always had a kind word to say.*

## Love does not envy

*Humility is defined as: Authentic/ Not prideful or arrogant. In fact, the root of the word humility is humus, meaning earth. Pop was indeed grounded and humble, despite him making Staff Sergeant in two years in the Korean War while serving as a crew chief.*

## Love does not boast

*Respectful is defined as: Treating others as important, and with dignity and respect. His time spent as a jailer again comes to mind and speaking Italian/ Spanish mix to some of the folks who found themselves in Collier County Jail.*

## Love is not self-seeking

*Selfless is defined as: Meeting the needs of others. He always thought of himself less and others more.*


## Love is not easily angered

*Forgiving is defined as: Giving up resentment when wronged. Let it go. Or, forgive those to whom Pop referred to as woodchucks.*


## Love rejoices with the truth

*Honesty is defined as: Free from Deception/ Accountability. [Guy in the Glass]. Hug **and** Spank. People of character tell the truth. [You're killin' me Smalls]. Address the gap(s). Be a Truth Teller — "To be honest with you Frank..."*


## Love always perseveres

*Commitment is defined as: Determination / Courage to follow through [From the Latin, cors, cordis, meaning heart]*
    *Nothing living stays the same*
    *He also reminded us that if you don't change the direction, you'll end up exactly where you're headed*
    *He knew that he had to practice these values, and set a proper example for others to follow*
    *We are indeed part of all that we've met. Think that given*

*his time as a manager at Victory Supermarket in upstate New York, he would agree with the analogy that we're either green and growing or ripe and rotting.*

*Let me re-read the Bible verse. Instead of Love, insert Pop/ Poppy/ George or how you referred to him, I will use Poppy:*

*Poppy was patient*
*Poppy was kind*
*Poppy was not envious*
*Poppy did not boast*
*Poppy was not rude*
*Poppy was not self-seeking*
*Poppy was not easily angered*
*Poppy kept no record of wrongs*
*Poppy did not delight in evil*
*Poppy rejoiced with the truth*
*Poppy always protected us*
*Poppy always trusted others*
*Poppy always hoped*
*Poppy always persevered*
*Poppy never failed.*

*Let us learn from his love that he exemplified.*
*Lastly, I am confident he is now with Peg and God for eternity.*

*Semper Fi.*
*We have the watch.*

Back Azimuths

# Personal Reflection

- One not only marries the spouse but also marries into a family. That family becomes part of you.
- Substitute the name of someone who is near and dear to you for the word love in 1 Corinthians 13:4-8. Then read it aloud. Or, if you would like to become more self-aware, substitute your name for love, and see if it is true.

_____ is patient
_____ is kind.
_____ does not envy
_____ does not boast
_____ is not proud.
_____ does not dishonor others
_____ is not self-seeking
_____ is not easily angered
_____ keeps no record of wrongs.
_____ does not delight in evil but rejoices with the truth.
_____ always protects
_____ always trusts
_____ always hopes
_____ always perseveres
_____ never fails

## Contemplate

Who is a partner or are partners in your life?

_____
_____
_____
_____
_____

What are the qualities that you bring to that partnership?

_____
_____
_____
_____
_____

What do you receive from that partnership?

_____
_____
_____
_____
_____

# Friendship

One joined in mutual benevolence, not ordinarily applied to lover or relatives, but of senses.

**Insight:** Luke 10:30-37.

*A man was going down from Jerusalem to Jericho, when he fell into the hands of robbers. They stripped him of his clothes, beat him and went away, leaving him half dead with no clothes. A priest happened to be going down the same road, and when he saw the man, he passed by on the other side. So too, a Levite, when he came to the place and saw him, passed by on the other side. But a Samaritan, as he traveled, came where the man was; and when he saw him, he took pity on him. He went to him and bandaged his wounds, pouring on oil and wine. Then he put the man on his own donkey, took him to an inn and took care of him. The next day he took out two silver coins and gave them to the innkeeper. 'Look after him,' he said, 'and when I return, I will reimburse you for any extra expense you may have.'*

"The road from Jerusalem to Jericho was notoriously dangerous. Narrow, steep and rocky, with sudden twists and turns, it was the perfect hunting ground for robbers to attack the merchants and travelers who frequented it. It is no wonder it was called 'The Bloody Road' or 'The Red Way'. The first hearers of this story knew the trek was a treacherous, risky highway to travel." [12]

**Inspire:**
Who is my enemy?
Who is my friend?
What if my enemy becomes my friend?

Although this verse is referred to as a Good Samaritan, for those who have been placed in harm's way, it is a paradox of sorts. I am reminded of F. Scott Fitzgerald, the author of *The Great Gatsby*, who stated, "The truest mark of intelligence is the ability to retain two diametrically opposed ideas in one's mind, and still retain the ability to function."[13]

**Ignite:** Genius of the 'and.' The Good Samaritan.[14]

---

12. Roger H. Nye. The Challenge of Command. Avery Publishing Group, Inc.; Wayne, NJ. 1986. 122

13. The truest mark of true intelligence is the ability to retain two diametrically opposed ideas in one's mind, and still retain the ability to function. Retrieved January 5, 2020 from https://quoteinvestigator.com/2020/01/05/intelligence.

14. The Good Samaritan. Retrieved December 19, 2008 from https://cartoonchurch.com/content/cc/the-good-samaritan/.

15, 16

The following are some excerpts from a paper written while I was a student at The US Naval War College entitled, *21st Century Soldier: Good Samaritan or Spartan?* The title stemmed from my experiences as a Soldier and to a chapter in the book by Roger Nye titled, *The Challenge of Command.*

In Nye's *Challenge of Command*, the author relates the New Testament Parable of the Good Samaritan. He used an example

---

15. Soldier comforts dying Iraqi girl. Retrieved December 20, 2008, from http://cellar.org/showthread.php?t=8285.

16. Soldiers in Iraq. Retrieved December 20, 2008 from https://www.nytimes.com/2008/04/18/world/middleeast/18sadrcity.html.

of a priest teaching this parable to cadets at West Point in the 1950s. The priest retold the Good Samaritan parable, and then went on to proclaim that if a Soldier was stationed on the road from Jerusalem to Jericho, this parable would not have to be taught: for the Soldier would understand the concept of duty, and never allow the beating and robbing of another to happen. Everyone left the chapel feeling great about their service and duty. The author then stated that the priest did not elaborate fully on the parable. [17]

What if the Rules of Engagement (ROE) were vague, or stated that the discharge of a weapon was for self-protection only? "What if the robbers were better armed, would the Soldier(s) allow the robbery to occur, or would the Soldier then be tempted to join in the plundering? What, if anything, will cause the Soldier to resist such temptations?"[18]

Some 21st Century Soldiers may indeed be tempted, as not all completely understand their role while deployed. In accordance with the U.S. Army's Soldier's Creed, a Soldier "stands ready to deploy, engage [in order to] and destroy the enemies of the United States in close combat."[19]

On one hand, this may correspond to the definition of a Spartan, as "a person of great courage and self-discipline." Conversely, in the current irregular warfare fight, it contrasts with the concept of a Good Samaritan, who is defined as "a person who is generous in helping those in distress." So, a 21st Century Soldier is expected to be both a Good Samaritan as well as a Spartan, and

---

17. Nye. 122.
18. Ibid.
19. Soldier's Creed, Retrieved January 10, 2009, from https://www.army.mil/values/soldiers.html.

to do both extremely well. Below are thoughts that I consider in understanding the differences:

## Good Samaritan

- Friendly
- Significant
- Mindset: Who is my neighbor? I must help him
- Education: Learn and (subsequently) Live (Educationally based)
- Unarmed
- Understanding
- Worldly
- Motive
- Values others

## Spartan

- Warrior
- Successful
- Who is my enemy? I must kill him
- Training: Live and Learn (Experienced based)
- Armed
- Unsympathetic
- Protective
- Results
- Values the state

Hence, the inherent conflict that 21st Century Soldiers and leaders find themselves is trying to understand how to be both Samaritan and Spartan for the violent, uncertain, complex, and ambiguous wartime environment. Similar to the Good Samaritan parable, this was the case in the initial 2003 invasion in Iraq, when 21st Century Soldiers had to confront the enemy who then became their neighbor (in the form of the new Iraqi Army).

It is my experience while training and leading 21st Century Soldiers prior to, during, and post deployment, that they constantly ask themselves, "What was my role? How does what I'm doing fit in to the big picture?" "I could do that?" Leaders have to be able to explain clearly and succinctly the task and purpose to their subordinates, as "they don't know what they don't know."

\* \* \*

If a 21st Century Soldier is presented with this parable, there is something more than law, custom, good behavior, and morality at stake. The 21st Century Soldier has to understand both the culture and the context to which he is assigned, and the leader has to convey the proper process involved. In this case, the Jews hated the Samaritans, which I compare to the Iraqi Sunni / Shia rift. Also, the terrain and environment influenced where the person was robbed and beaten. So, the 21st Century Soldier not only has to be properly trained in both the technical and tactical aspects of the job—location, employment of Soldiers, weapons, and equipment—but also in the culture, the why of the deployment, and to balance compassion with the Rules of Engagement (ROE).

What would be the 21st Century Soldiers' ROE along this stretch of road? Would they have been able to stop the mugging and beating from occurring? Would the units' values be different from the indigenous people? Or would it have been similar to coalition forces watching the looting take place after the fall of Baghdad in 2003? The Three General Orders that all Soldiers are taught do not address what to do.[20]

Perhaps, the unit's orders may include protection of citizens and prevention of such acts from occurring, while allowing for force protection.

\* \* \*

The art behind the science of warfighting involves embracing values and virtues and developing a willingness to work with they who were once former enemies, and values and virtues can serve 21st Century Soldiers in the 'unknowns.' A good approach to balancing being a Good Samaritan / Spartan, is to possess a sense of intellectual humility, and have a self-assessment attitude of "every day I realize how much there is that I do not know." The best leaders are lifelong learners, are continually learning, reading, and adapting, and are never satisfied with the status quo, or that their current duty assignment is just a temporary step to the next level. Indeed, there remains a sense of ambition in these leaders; however, "ambition is to be commended if it leads to professionalism and is to be condemned if it leads to careerism."[21]

---

20. 3 General Orders. Retrieved December 22, 2008 from https://www.armystudyguide.com/content/Prep_For_Basic_Training/Prep_for_basic_general_information/3-general-orders.shtml. 1st General Order: "I will guard everything within the limits of my post and quit my post only when properly relieved." 2nd General Order: "I will obey my special orders and perform all of my duties in a military manner." 3rd General Order: "I will report violations of my special orders, emergencies, and anything not covered in my instructions, to the commander of the relief.

21. James H. Toner. *Morals Under the Gun. The Cardinal Virtues, Military Ethics, and American Society*. The University of Kentucky Press, Lexington, Kentucky. 2000. 32.

## Personal Reflection

- 21st Century Soldiers and leaders use moral habituation to find a moral compass
- In our lives, it is best to emphasize the 1st Person Plural (we, us, ours), not 1st person singular (I, me).
- Take care of "them."

## Contemplate

In what way have you ever been placed in a position of a Good Samaritan?

_____
_____
_____
_____
_____

Do you always treat others with dignity and respect? Why or why not?

_____
_____
_____
_____
_____

What would you do if you were stationed on the road from Jerusalem to Jericho?

_____
_____
_____
_____
_____

# Leadership

Direction, guidance. Influencing others within a given context.

**Insight:** Proverbs 22:6.

*"Train the young in the way they should go; even when old, they will not swerve from it."*

Yes, parents are our first teachers, and first leaders that we follow. Pope Paul VI, in the *Gravissium Educationis*, wrote that, "The role of parents in education is of such importance that it is almost impossible to provide an adequate substitute."[22] Those who raise us certainly want what is best for us, although there are times when we certainly do not think that is the case. It is part of growing and learning.

**Inspire:** Around your house, or office, pick up something that has significant meaning to you. I learned this icebreaker technique from an Emotional Intelligence (EQ-i) certification in July 2020.[23] The training and certification was being done via Zoom

---

22. *Gravissium Educationis*. Pope Paul VI. 1965.
23. Burns Personal Notes.

due to COVID-19 protocols. The participants were asked to look around their desk and find something that had significant meaning to them. Then, when called upon, we were to share what that particular item means to them. I selected a wedge, a simple tool, and offered why it has such meaning to me (for further explanation, please see pp 144, on Workmanship).

**Ignite:** Setting a personal example of excellence in word and deed.

*October 2007, Baghdad, Iraq. 6th Iraqi Army Division Military Transition Team (MiTT).*

Following friendship, below are some additional thoughts on leadership from *21st Century Soldier: Good Samaritan or Spartan?"*

> Not to feel exasperated or defeated or despondent because your days aren't packed with wise and moral actions. But to get back up when you fail, to celebrate behaving like a human — however imperfectly — and fully embrace the pursuit you've embarked on.
> 
> —**Marcus Aurelius**

I can offer "no magic can of spinach,"[24] or "no quick victories or magic formulas."[25] The secret is that there is no secret. Certainly, the addition of the cardinal virtues to complement Army values will provide additional clarity (content) in order for 21st Century Soldiers and leaders to understand the context of a given situation and assess in the process of leading. As senior leaders we must know well the four cardinal virtues and how to apply them to whateverthreat that the Armed Services face. I assert that moral / ethical decision making needs to be added to each Professional Military Education curriculum from junior enlisted to senior leaders, but it needs to be taught by the right people. James Toner, a professor at the Air War College, echoed this thought of how to apply this in his book, *Morals Under the Gun*, when he wrote that "Teaching, directly or indirectly, is also the life's worth of all armed forces officers,"[26] and it is also a "drawing out from the mind of the student the knowledge that is already there."[27] Perhaps there is this need for what Thucydides called *kataphronesis*, or "an arrogant hauteur with regard to its military capability."[28] Although this trait

---

24. *popeye syndrome*. (2008). In Runner's World Online. Retrieved December 23, 2008 from http://www.johnbingham.com/cc_00_02_popeye.html "One of my favorites was Popeye. Of all the heroes on TV, he seemed to have the best system. Any time he was in trouble, [which nearly always centered and Bluto's over attention to Olive Oil] all he had to do was reach into his shirt, pull out a can of spinach, squeeze it into the air, and catch it in his mouth. PRESTO. Instant muscles, instant strength, instant solution…The only magic in my life as a runner was the magic of consistency. If I was willing to do the work, even when I couldn't see the results immediately, I was ultimately rewarded. I understand myself well enough to know that I'm still looking for that can of spinach. I scoured the articles and books for some previously unknown potion that will speed up my transition."

25. Fr. Daniel L. Mode. *Grunt Padre, The Service & Sacrifice of Father Vincent Robert Capodanno, Vietnam 1966-67*. CMJ Marian Publishers. Oak Lawn, IL. 2000. 139.

26. *Toner, Morals Under the Gun*. 94.

27. Joseph G. Brennan. *Foundations of Moral Obligations. The Stockdale Course*. Naval War College Press: Newport, RI. 1992. 206.

28. Will Desmond. *The hybris of Socrates: A Platonic 'revaluation of values' in the Symposi*. Retrieved 4 February 2009, 43, from http://eprints.nuim.ie/930/1/8._Desmond_-_The_Hybris_of_Socrates.pdf.

is not always appreciated from junior leaders, it is a trait that is necessary for senior leaders but should be blended with the phrase *ensenar deleitando*—or to teach so that learning is enjoyable.[29]

Besides understanding the cardinal virtues and how they complement the Army values (content), the U.S. Army needs to improve its situational and cultural awareness training (context). With the recent deployments to Asia, the U.S. Army has often applied a Western mindset to an Eastern problem. We need to understand and emphasize how attitudes and cultural beliefs of opposing ethnic groups affect each other.[30] We can do this by focusing on building Soldiers from the 'skin in'—the same way it is done with teaching Army values to Initial Military Training (IMT) Soldiers—versus from the 'skin out' or just piling hi-tech gear such as Oakley sunglasses, slick helmets, digitized uniforms, and new weapons on Soldiers. This 'skin in' focus is how values and virtues are inculcated into the core of a Soldier. The new equipment or kit does not make the Soldier, but instead, repetitive training / muscle memory on basic Soldier skills, including values and virtues, does. This 'skin-in' approach was recognized by an obscure Army major (George Patton) in 1933, when he wrote in a treatise entitled *Success In War*, "It's the gleam in the eye of the attacker and not the glitter of the bayonet that breaks the line, yet volumes are devoted to armament, and pages to inspiration."[31]

There are other ways to improve and understand the concept of duty. One way is to read and study biographies and case studies of

---

29. John H. Elliott. *Spain and Its World*, 1500-1700. Yale University Press, Hartford, CT. 1990. 170.

30. Anthony E. Hartle. *Moral Issues in Military Decision Making*. University Press of Kansas, Leavenworth, KS. 2004. 215.

31. Patton Quote. As found in J. William Gallup, *Final Argument: That Eloquence of Diction; That Poetry of Imagination; That Brilliance of Metaphor*. The Nebraska Lawyer, July 2006. Retrieved 20 December, 2008 from http://www.nebar.com/pdfs/nelawyer/2006/July%2006/0706d.pdf.

great leaders, specifically in relation to the concept of duty or piety, although while deployed, this proves difficult. Besides working 14-18 hours per day, one must balance exercise, praying, eating, and reading [32] (and, while not deployed, family time has to be balanced). This will integrate the 21st Century Soldiers' and leaders' education in content, context, and processes. Besides building a strong virtue and value foundation at the various Professional Military Education (PME, where service members receive development, training and development through formal schools, colleges, university, internships, etc.), leaders' strategic communications should include following its own doctrine. Field Manual (FM) 6-22 offers many examples, and how to habituate making the right moral / ethical decision in leaders and subordinates, ranging from having a flexible mindset in small group discussion on ethical decisions to blogging and emailing with members of the command. Also, the case studies that are currently taught to deploying Soldiers by Staff Judge Advocate officers should instead be taught by leaders who can relate the scenario to values and virtues, not just say "the Rules of Engagement (ROE) does not allow it."[33] I view this as teaching moral courage, and it may assist in finding the cardinal virtues in "the action to make the world meet their standards"[34] as was referred to by Rear Admiral (RADM) James B. Stockdale in his reference to the action of Medal of Honor recipients, "and is not far from Aristotle's ideal of somewhere between the gods and humans."[35] I agree with Pete Mansoor, former USMA professor as well as a former Army brigade commander in Iraq, who argued

---

32. George Casey. *Transition Team Briefing*. Camp Taji, Iraq. November 2006.

33. Burns Personal Notes.

34. James B. Stockdale. Foundations of Moral Obligation; The Stockdale Course. *Heroes and Heroism*. 23.

35. Ibid. 26.

in *Baghdad at Sunrise,* for a need to focus more on humanities and a true liberal arts education instead of focusing on technical degrees and training such as engineering and science taught at some of the pre-commissioning sources and PME.[36] Or as Don Snider, a USMA history professor, alluded to at the 2007 Ethics Consultation at Fort Jackson, SC, that "there is more to developing Soldiers than education and training."[37] I believe that what this development process entails could be interpreted as habituation.

Those who have returned from deployments or experienced trauma have an obligation to share their experiences, in order to reinforce moral and ethical choices and habituation. Having recently returned from OIF, as well as having been present at the Pentagon on 9-11, I can empathize with Kimberly Dozier, a CBS news reporter, who was wounded in Iraq:

> Throughout the first six months, there was the ever-present wallop of grief and guilt that comes from surviving when those around you have died. Along with the physical battle isthe one in your heart and soul—making sure memories of the trauma and violence, and the grief that follows, do not end up haunting you for the rest of time. After you've dealt with your own inner battle, then have to deal with the prejudices of an American public (your own friends included) who assume going through tragedy leaves you some sort of scarred-for-life walking time bomb.[38]

Understanding the concepts that are found in the cardinal vir-

---

36. Pete Mansoor. *Baghdad at Sunrise.* Yale University Press, New Haven and London. 2008. 347.
37. Don Snider. *Ethics and the Human Development of the Soldier Spirit,* The Army Chaplaincy. Spring-Summer 2008. 23-34.
38. Kimberly Dozier, *Technically I Was Dead.* Retrieved 30 December 29 2008, from http://www.newsweek.com/id/137513.

tues will assist in working through these lessons. It will also ensure that subordinates understand them and do the right thing when they are confronted with such circumstances. Recently, USMC General Mattis was asked how he was able to make a decision in 10 minutes to give an order to arrest insurgents who were attending a wedding stated, "It did not take me 10 minutes to make that decision. It took me 34 years and 10 minutes."[39] It was habituation, and a strong moral compass that allowed General Mattis to make that decision.

21st Century Soldiers and leaders use moral habituation to find a moral compass. General MacArthur spoke of this moral compass when he stated, "Last, but by no means least, courage—moral courage, the courage of one's convictions, the courage to see things through. The world is in a constant conspiracy against the brave. It's the age-old struggle—the roar of the crowd on one side and the voice of your conscience on the other."[40] Also, included in Pete Mansoor's book *Baghdad At Sunrise*, he relates how, upon return from Iraq, he suggested to a mother with whom he was talking that her son should look into the United States Military Academy (USMA). She replied with, "Oh no, we have much higher hopes for our son. But you just keep on doing what you're doing, though. We need people like you."[41] We need to ensure that these people and those like them are the ones who educate the sheepdogs in the art of leadership. It remains that "true authority comes not from power to enforce but from the ability to inspire."[42]

---

39. James Mattis, Retrieved December 29, 2008, from http://obsidianwings.blogs.com/obsidian_wings/2006/08/lt_gen_james_ma.html.

40. MacArthur quote. Retrieved on December 29, 2008, from http://www.quoteopia.com/famous.php?quotesby=douglasmacarthur.

41. Mansoor. *Baghdad at Sunrise*. 352.

42. Connections. Retrieved January 30, 2009 from http://www.connections-mediaworks.com/sundaygospel.html#feb1.

## Conclusion

Although moral courage—including maturity, professionalism, ethics, morals, judgment, and discipline—is necessary and very much needed, desired and essential for the 21st Century Soldier and leader alike, it remains difficult to educate and to execute. As a senior leader, I need to build upon the values training taught during Initial Military Training, the use of AARs to drive home lessons learned, and emphasize professional reading of moral and ethical case studies in Soldiers' experiential education. It is not only to understand the values and virtues—the content, but also the environment to where one may be deployed—the context, as well as the process required to inspire the values and virtues in others. By fully understanding Army values and how they are complemented by the cardinal virtues to build a firm moral and ethical foundation and develop a moral compass, I can find, teach, and educate others in the proper balance betweena Good Samaritan and Spartan. By finding this balance we will avoid the words of Sam Damon, from Anton Myrer's classic *Once an Eagle*, "If it comes down to a choice between being a good Soldier and a good human being, be a good human being."[43] So, if I was stationed on 'The Bloody Road', I would take action and encourage others to take action, and perhaps there would indeed be a *kairos* moment—a cosmically meaningful moment outside of linear time[44]—when we would choose to enter the moral sphere of another.

Finally, we will also be heeding well the words of Xenophon, in *The Anabasis of Cyrus:*

---

43. Anton Myrer, *Once An Eagle*, Harper Collins Publishers; New York, NY.
44. *Rick Rescorla*. Retrieved February 9, 2009, from https://www.cmohs.org/citizen-honors/rick-rescorla

## Back Azimuths

For my part, men, I have pondered also this, that regarding all those who crave staying alive through wars in whatever way they can, these for the most part die both badly and shamefully; but all those who know that death is common to and necessary for all human beings, and compete over dying nobly, these I see somehow arriving more often into old age and, for as long as they live, passing their time more happily [45]

---

45. Xenophon. *The Anabasis of Cyrus*. Translated and annotated by Wayne Ambler. Cornell University Press. 2008. Book 3, chapter 2, line 44.

## Personal Reflection

- We are standing on the shoulders of the giants who came before us, and the example and standards that they set for us.
- Not every leader possesses qualities that we desire to emulate.
- Do we view the past though a 21st Century lens?

## Contemplate

Describe the best qualities of a leader.
_____
_____
_____
_____
_____


What are your strongest leadership traits?
_____
_____
_____
_____
_____


How can you use your strengths to leverage your weak traits?
_____
_____
_____
_____
_____

# Marksmanship

One skilled at shooting or aiming.

**Insight:** 1 Samuel 17.

> *Then he took his staff in his hand, chose five smooth stones from the stream, put them in the pouch of his shepherd's bag and, with his sling in his hand, approached the Philistine.*

In his book *David and Goliath*, the author Malcolm Gladwell argues that David was actually the underdog in this story.[46] David had previously killed both lions and bears with the use of his sling and stone. Gladwell further argues that the giant Goliath actually had a pituitary gland growth issue which caused him to grow so large, and also to lose some of his sight. If you recall, Goliath uses a walking stick, has a guide, and claims to see two people approaching. Nonetheless, the force of the stone that David slings and hits Goliath does the damage to Goliath, who eventually falls and is beheaded by David. In order to be as accurate as David was with

---

46. David and Goliath: Underdogs, Misfits, and the Art of Battling Giants, Malcolm Gladwell. 2013.

his sling and stone, he had to have put in the time and effort to improve his marksmanship skills.

**Inspire:** From 2004-06, early on in training at Army basic military training at Fort Benning, Georgia, besides the mandatory classes on the Uniform Code of Military Justice (UCMJ) and Law of Land Warfare, Infantry Enlisted Soldiers were shown short excerpts from recent films in order to establish an ethical / moral foundation, as from my experience, not every Soldier has a firm background prior to coming into the Army. These film excerpts showed how a particular value can relate to something that the Soldier may have already seen or experienced. The senior officer in the unit (battalion commander) taught these classes, with the entire cadre present, and offered Socratic questions as a means of shaping each Soldier's moral compass. This initial values training built the Soldiers' concept of duty, or a willingness to commit to a larger cause, and implies a sense of belonging and togetherness. It was a necessary first step in the inculcation and habituation, or doing the right thing, in the right manner, for the right reasons. This was in line with Aristotle's thought, "We are what we repeatedly do. Excellence, therefore, is not an act, but a habit."[47]

Also, during my tenure at Fort Benning, we taught Army Values through short film clips. For example, from the film, *The Patriot*, we used the phrase, "Aim small, miss small."[48]

The four marksmanship fundamentals ingrained into Soldiers:
1. Steady position
2. Sight Picture/ alignment
3. Breathing

---

47. Aristotle Quote. Retrieved December 29, 2008 from https://medium.com/the-mission/my-favourite-quote-of-all-time-is-a-misattribution-66356f22843d
48. Emmerich, Roland. The Patriot. Columbia Pictures. 2000.

## 4. Trigger Squeeze [49]

Although there are four fundamentals, we are reminded of the rules of five: we have five senses, five tastes, can see five colors, five musical notes, and there were five stones that David retrieved from the stream prior to slaying Goliath. In lieu of the trigger squeeze, David may have used wrist snap and follow through.

**Ignite:** Attention to detail.

*Fort Benning, Georgia, May 2005. 1st Battalion, 50th Infantry Regiment Memorial. The names on the stones are those who lost their lives in Vietnam.*

We are reminded daily that we all may have Dory (from the film *Finding Nemo*) moments, when grocery shopping, locking the keys inside car, or forgetting one's keys or to lock the door, etc. We

---

49. Four Marksmanship Fundamentals. Retrieved December 29, 2008 from https://study.com/academy/lesson/the-four-fundamentals-of-marksmanship.html.

would like to be able to experience less of these types of moments and instead have moments that enrich our lives.

With that, we would like to turn *chronos* into *kairos* moments. One has to put in the quantitative time in order to have qualitative moments. As we tend to be fixated on the quick fix, we often do not desire to put the necessary effort into praying, readings, exercising, sleeping, or thinking. It is more than just muscle memory.

Below are some thoughts from One Station Unit Training (OSUT) Graduation Ceremony at Fort Benning, Georgia. I attempted to inspire in them how the past 14 weeks of training has improved their skills, especially marksmanship, and made them ready to be sent where the country may need them. Also, tied into this is the thought that at times we have pass out lead, and times we have to pass out lead.

*\*\*\**

*Thank you for attending our graduation ceremony this great Infantry morning. Hooah!!*

*I would like to recognize and thank the hardest working band in the Army, Benning's own, for their participation and their professional expertise this morning. Please join me in a round of applause for the Infantry Band.*

*The support given by 29th Infantry Regiment here today, and on all the ranges for the past 14 weeks — well done — it's a team of teams here @ Fort Benning, you have played a tremendous part in the graduation today. [Applause].*

*Having stood on parade more than a few times over the past few years, I'm sure the Soldiers standing out in front of us really want to hear only three words, "PASS IN REVIEW." We'll get to that soon, hang in there.*

## Back Azimuths

*It's been said that the purpose of a Guest Speaker at a graduation exercise is equivalent to the corpse at an Irish wake—both are expected for the ceremony, but neither is required to say too much. Folks will not long remember what any guest speaker says this morning (maybe that joke), as today is about the Soldiers standing before us—these Infantrymen.*

*I am here to attempt to give these Infantrymen a proper Send off from their Initial Entry Training. But "Unhappily," I, just as GEN Douglas MacArthur stated, "I possess neither that eloquence of diction, that poetry of imagination, nor that brilliance of metaphor,"*[50] *to do these Soldiers justice by my words this morning.*

*These young men have what it takes to join our band of brothers—the ranks of the U. S. Army's Infantry. In joining our ranks, they join an elite segment of the American population. In order to protect this great nation of over several hundred million, there are only 44 thousand enlisted Infantry soldiers. These 44 thousand Warriors, are very similar to that small band of Spartans at Thermopylae, standing between us and the enemy*

*These young men—these Infantrymen—were trained by their Drill Sergeants. These new Infantrymen will not long remember their battalion commanders' names, or the names of their Company Commanders or First Sergeants—but they will always remember the name of their Drill Sergeant (DS). It is burned into their memory as if with fire—that is the way it has always been and the way it must always be. You veterans out there, you remember their names, don't you? For me it was DS Piedrata and DS Taylor. Just as we will not forget our*

---

50. Douglas C. MacArthur, Duty Honor, Country, May 12 1962, Speech given at United States Military Academy (USMA), West Point, NY.

*Drill Sergeants, the Soldiers standing before you today will never forget men like DS Benjamin, DS Torres, and DS Stoen. DSs whose time here—after two or more years on the trail—is done. Like these Infantrymen, our departing DSs return to the field Army to join those 44 thousand Warriors deployed on missions around the world. The DSs' presence here assures us that these Infantrymen are ready and equal to the task. Please join me in a round of applause for the Drill Sergeants and for their service to our nation.*

*The world situation that awaits these Soldiers is entirely different that the world situation when some of us joined the Army. After WW II, we were in the Cold War for about 44 years — until the fall of the Berlin Wall and the collapse of Soviet Union in 1989. Some of us were in Germany at the time, forward deployed where, decades earlier, members of the Greatest Generation had fought and won. It was a known enemy; there was a wall between us. We had something called the General Defense Plan, or GDP, of Europe. Everything was pre-planned, from our time of alert, going to a local dispersal area, training, then deploying to the positions along the East German border. Everything was time phased; we had a set plan of action. All our fighting positions were pre-determined, in a battle book, we knew the enemy, its strengths and weakness, and from where they would attack. There was not much flexibility or innovation.*

*I compare that "Cold War" Soldier mentality vs. 21st Century Warrior as comparing football to rugby, respectively. Viewed from above, both football and rugby are very similar, as the teams make their way across the field or pitch. In American football, as with Cold War tactics, we have a playbook (In Desert Shield / Storm alone, there were at least 76 Contingency Plans written); specialists who perform specific fixed functions or roles; we blow the whistle upon completion of each play; there is time — a huddle — to make plans for each play; the other team may not get the ball until you turn it over on downs; there is a static piece to the line of scrimmage, Commands are "Ready, set, hut"; there are forward passes; there are pre-determined plays, and not many audibles. In rugby, the action is fluid, dynamic, non-stop, there is no specialization; anyone can score; there is a whistle only if there is a serious infraction. Everyone is self-aware and adaptable, as anyone can kick, punt, pass, and score. You know the strengths / weaknesses of fellow players better; you are more supportive players.*

*So today, the Global War on Terror requires us to pass out bread off the back of a truck one moment and to pass out lead from the barrels of our weapons the next. Soldiers have to be self-aware and adaptable, there is no pre-determined rhythm — everything is fluid and dynamic, as well as violent, uncertain, complex, and often ambiguous. These Soldiers must be confident and competent and possess a great deal of character — I can assure you, these Soldiers before you today possess those traits and then some. One of the more remarkable traits that these Soldiers now possess is marksmanship, or how to pass out lead.*

*They may have told you, the Soldiers before you have had their M4 rifles by their side with them since the first 72 hours of being assigned here. They have inculcated into their muscle memory the four principles of steady position, sight picture / alignment, breathing, and trigger squeeze. They have fired well over a thousand rounds through their rifles: From learning assembly and disassembly, functionality, zeroing, familiarization, field fire, record fire, qualification, Nuclear Biological and Chemical firing, night fire with night vision goggles, short range marksmanship, Buddy Team live Fire, and convoy live fire, they have worked hard at a worthwhile task—becoming a Soldier.*

*Former President Teddy Roosevelt once said, "The best prize that life offers, is the chance to work hard, at work, worth doing."[51] Let there be no doubt, you will work hard, but there is no other work as worthy as Soldiering.*

*Play the Game—Mailed Foot—We Guard.*
*Thank You.*

---

51. Teddy Roosevelt quote, Retrieved 2005, June 10, 2005 from https://www.forbes.com/quotes/8980/.

## Personal Reflection

- Have faith in God.
- Learn about yourself, and practice until it becomes ingrained into you as muscle memory

## Contemplate

What is an example of an underdog in your life?

_____
_____
_____
_____
_____

What is that skill, outside your comfort zone, that you want to learn and practice until it becomes muscle memory?

_____
_____
_____
_____
_____

Have you invested the necessary quantity of time (*chronos*) in order to have qualitative (*kairos*) moments?

_____
_____
_____
_____
_____

# Followership

To go or come after (a person or other object in motion); to move behind in the same direction.

**Insight:** Isaiah 6:8.

*"Then I heard the voice of the Lord saying, "Whom shall I send? Who will go for us?" "Here I am;" I said, "send me!"*

I used this in a farewell speech to graduating Soldiers from Initial Entry Training. I had read an article online about going away and coincided with the graduation ceremony. To me is describes the essence of followership:

Lastly, to the Soldiers who are going away. I want to say something to you. You know, you don't just go away. I don't like the word 'GO'. 'GO' kind of means you just leave, you're untethered, and you break away from the moorings and just float around out there. Soldiers don't GO, we're 'SENT'. Being 'SENT' has a whole different connotation. 'SENT' means you got support. 'SENT' means you've got a home. 'SENT' means you can always come back. Being 'SENT' means people love you. 'SENT' means taking on a cause beyond yourself. It means you go out like a Warrior because you've got something to do. And when you get it done, you come back to your home, family, and friends, because they're all there waiting for you. Man, what a feeling that is.

**Inspire:** Don't Volunteer. That's what we're told. We tend to want to remain in our comfort zone. There, we remain callous, often are condescending to others, and unwilling to change. If we do change, we tend to be hesitant. There are difficult conversations to be had. There are times we do not want to be outside in bad weather, in uncomfortable situations, being with others, embracing the suck. Nonetheless, the hard times are what best shape and develops our character.

**Ignite:** The Process.

### Gaius Valerius Catullus
### Poem No. 101

Multas per gentes et multa per aequora vectus
advenio has miseras, frater, ad inferias,
ut te postremo donarem munere mortis
et mutam nequiquam alloquerer cinerem.
quandoquidem fortuna mihi tete abstulit ipsum.
heu miser indigne frater adempte mihi,
nunc tamen interea haec, prisco quae more parentum
tradita sunt tristi munere ad inferias,
accipe fraterno multum manantia fletu,
atque in perpetuum, frater, ave atque vale.

*Ave Atque Vale, by Catullus.* [52]

---

52. Ave Atque Vale., Catullus, Retrieved December 12, 2020 from https://www.classicstuition.co.uk/catullus-poem-no-7-read-in-latin-by-sean-gabb/.

We often hear coaches and teachers claim that it's all about 'The Process.' John Wooden, the legendary coach of UCLA men's basketball said that what he missed the most about being a coach? The practices. I too, echo this sentiment.

Followership and Leadership are two sides of the same coin. What? I believe that they complement each other and should not necessarily compete against each other. I gave the below thoughts during a farewell / retirement dinner for Brigadier General (BG) James C. Yarbrough and his wife at Fort Polk, LA in January 2011. At the end of dinner, I gave a translation of the *Ave Atque Vale* poem written by Catullus. Being an Infantryman, it was a bit outside my comfort zone, as combat arms officers are often not considered scholars or academicians.

\* \* \*

*Thank you, Cathy Yarbrough, and Training Audio Support Center (TASC) for the family video.*

*Thank you, Julia Yarbrough, representing the 4th Generation to serve.*

*Two words best describe video: NICE BASS.*

*Thank on-post folks, esp. 4th Brigade, 10th Mountain Division spouses, as well as off-post civic leaders—testament to what Brigadier General (BG) has established in the community.*

*Dearly Beloved... Oops, hey Chaplain Waters, you left your speech up here. (throw away)*

*The First Noel... leftover again (throw away)*

*God is Great, Beer is Good, people are Crazy... OK, here we go*

The First Hail and Farewell, I'll get to that it a few minutes.

If General McChrystal was referred to as the Patton of Strategic Communications, I consider myself the Forrest Gump of speeches (in his reference to a box of chocolates) — you never know what you're gonna get.

When you get older in life, things get taken from you. It's part of life; only learn that when you start losing stuff or people...

As I told the Garrison Staff yesterday, my first image of BG Yarbrough is at Fort Benning, Georgia, in the field, with a Kevlar helmet, Body Armor, Modular Lightweight Load-carrying Equipment (MOLLE) vest, Camouflage on face and neck, teaching / coaching / mentoring on a Friday afternoon around 1600 —when no one else would be out. To put that in perspective, it's about an hour's drive from main post, young Captains don't always have the right grid on where they are located, all have to get camouflaged up and put on all the necessary gear. By the way, it's 90+ degrees and HEAT Category 5, you have to know what day that the Soldiers are in training, be able to speak to the Soldiers and leaders in a manner that only he can. So, this trait, this habit, was probably ingrained into him from some solid Non-Commissioned Officers (NCOs) when he was a young Lieutenant (in the Ranger Regiment as some here can attest), and I have consistently observed to this day. He has had this leadership trait ingrained in him, and it is clearly evident — be it at Fort Benning, Iraq, or here having been intimately and directly involved in making this installation earn the title "Home of Heroes."

I have been told that I should keep it simple tonight and **Speak in Threes**, so here it goes:

- *Best descriptors for both General and Mrs. Yarbrough: Passion, Action, Impact*
- *Boudreaux, Thibodeaux, Yarbrough...*
- *John Wayne, Johnny Cash, John Deere...*
- *Moe, Larry, Curley*

*Movies: Deliverance, The Waterboy, Southern Comfort, or Billy the Exterminator, Steel Magnolias, LA TV show Hunting Alligators*
- *Coach, Teach, Mentor*
- *Favorite "ing" words: we're working it; fishing, water skiing*

*Emergency Operations Center (EOC) Messages: Heat CAT III, Heat CAT IV, Heat Cat V*

*Commanding General Huddle Notes: Commander's Critical Information Requirements (CCIR). Certain folks would sit around his conference table in his office on MON mornings and give him updates. (Allegedly, and this is from the Operations Officer or G3, although I never heard him say this, but allegedly was heard after someone would give him an update on a topic), he would reply, That's CCIR, that's CCIR, That's CCIR*

## Other Fort Polk Memories

*Downtown: Witch Way to Main Street: Dressed up as a Gladiator (Spartacus, borrowing Post Command Sergeant Major's kit) and his bride, Cathy, as Cleopatra; operationalizing Army Community Covenant: School Development, Economic Development, Affordable & Quality Housing, Transportation, Land*

*Purchase Initiative (and all the legal wording that it entailed), and the Highway 467 Development.*

*Installation Management Command (IMCOM): we're broke, we're broke, we're broke, BUT, the G8 (Post Comptroller) has the money ($$), they just won't give it to us.*

*It's said that the best things said come last. People will talk for hours saying nothing much and then linger at the door with words that come with a rush from the heart. Perhaps the biggest lesson that he and Cathy have taught me, in word and in deed and I continue to be amazed by it, is that Character is permanent, Issues are transitory.*

*In the military, we have many traditions, one of which is called a Hail & Farewell. For some it is the first & last time that one will see the person, as Soldiers and families rotate through different Army units — be it Permanent Change of Station, End of Terminal Service, going away, or passing away. I used this at my first Hail & Farewell in Kirchgoens, Germany in 1990. Darlene probably has this better memorized than I. I also used this in a eulogy within a week of return from Iraq in February 2008 at my brother's funeral, so it has special meaning for me.*

*I'll read a translation of the original Hail & Farewell, which was written by a Latin poet, Catullus in 1st Century B.C. Catullus is well known for his erotic poetry; however, much to the chagrin of Colonel Stammer and the Operations Group, I will not recite any of that, which we were not allowed to read in Catholic school. Instead, one of the poems he is best known for is a serious poem, entitled Ave Atque Vale, which translates to Hail and Farewell. Catullus had lost his brother in a foreign war, in Asia Minor, or modern-day*

## Back Azimuths

*Turkey, just north of where we were together in Iraq. Catullus was inspired by a visit to his brother's grave. It was the first and last time that he had seen his brother, albeit via his graveside. I first translated this poem about 28 years ago, in a high school Latin class, with Sr. Mary Virginia, and have carried it around with me ever since. Although Catullus is addressing his brother in death, this is from where our tradition of Hail and Farewell stems:*

*Through many countries and over many seas*
*I have come, Brother, to these melancholy rites,*
*to show this final honor to the dead,*
*and speak to your silent ashes,*
*since now fate takes you, even you, from me.*
*Oh, Brother, ripped away from me so cruelly,*
*now at least take these last offerings, blessed*
*by the tradition of our parents, gifts to the dead.*
*Accept, by custom, what a brother's tears drown,*
*and, for eternity, Brother,* **Ave Atque Vale.**

Francis B. Burns

## Personal Reflection

- Yes, I believe that followership and leadership complement each other.
- What I try to follow in my life is Faith, Flag, Family, Friends, and Fun. And yes, they also complement each other.

## Contemplate

Who do you follow and why?
_____
_____
_____
_____
_____

What impression did you believe that you made on someone whom you met for the first time? For the last time?
_____
_____
_____
_____
_____

What is your calling? Your vocation?
_____
_____
_____
_____
_____

# Ambassadorship

(3) appointed or official messenger; plus...ship equals the office, position or function of an ambassador.

**Insight:** 2 Corinthians 5:20.

*"So we are ambassadors for Christ, as if God were appealing through us. We implore you on behalf of Christ, to be reconciled with God."*

I strive to live a life built upon Judeo-Christian values: the four cardinal virtues of prudence, justice, fortitude, and temperance, along with the theological virtues of faith, hope, and charity. I often fall short in my attempt to live up to these virtues and let down myself as well as others when I do not live up to them. For that I remain truly remorseful, and vow to continually improve upon my shortcomings.

**Inspire:** *Quo vadis?* Where are you going? This phrase is attributed to Peter, as he saw Jesus walking along The Appian Way to be crucified again. These words give Peter the courage to continue his Christian ministry in Rome, and to be crucified, although upside-down.

*Quid agis?* How are you doing? I use written communication as a means to convey thoughts, emotions, things that I am going through. While deployed, I wrote weekly emails to family and friends to let them know how I was doing. I thought that these weekly emails would offer a different perspective than one found or read in newspaper, online, in blogs, or listening to commentaries.

In a sense, the weekly emails were both therapeutic (letting others know how I am doing) and diagnostic (current assessment) to me. At my home, I have a box of letters that my father sent to my mother during WW II, prior to their marriage. Perhaps, I took a lesson or two from the sentiment found in their correspondence from the 1940s.

**Ignite:** Pride.

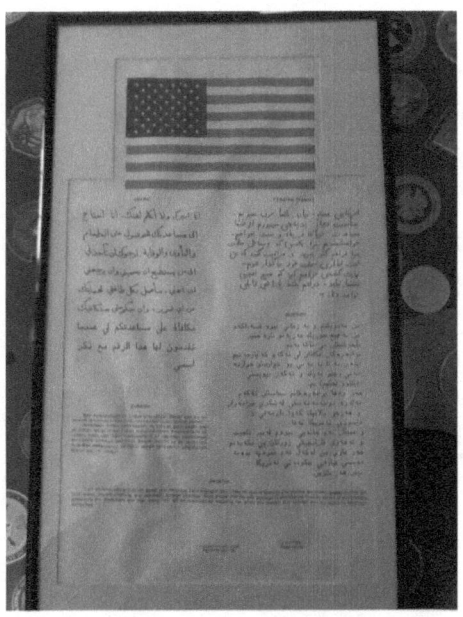

*2006, Baghdad, Iraq. Blood Chit. I carried this in Operation Iraqi Freedom (OIF) 06-08, while part of a Military Transition Team (MiTT), to assist in safe return and aid in case I was separated from my unit. In addition to the American flag, it has the following translated into Arabic. Persian (Farsi), Turkish, and Kurdish:*

I am an American and do not speak your language. I will not harm you! I bear no malice towards your people. My friend please provide me food, water, shelter, clothing, and necessary medical attention. Also, please provide safe passage to the nearest friendly forces of any country supporting the Americans and their allies. You will be rewarded for assisting me when you present this number and my name to American authorities.

We all have a sense of pride stemming from where we have

come. We often reach back for assurance on where we find ourselves.

I have used the first and last emails that I sent to family and friends while deployed to address ambassadorship. I knew what I was representing; yet, at the same time, I attempted to offer a personal connection on what I was going through at the time.

This is the first of weekly emails that I sent to family and friends. It is just a note that reads all is OK, I had just arrived in Baghdad (aka the big city).

—Original Message—

```
From: Burns, Francis LTC, 4/1 CAV MITT, Dep-
uty Chief [mailto:francis-burns@mnd-b.army.
mil]

Sent: Sunday, November 12, 2006 2:22 AM

To:
Subject: [U] In country
Classification: UNCLASSIFIED

All,

Am finally in the big city. New position is
the Deputy Senior Advisor for an Iraqi Divi-
sion HQs. Not in area where I was scheduled
to be. I was nominated to come down here.
Feel as if I was the player to be named lat-
er. Have only been here a few days. New mail-
ing address for a few months, anyway, is:
```

## Back Azimuths

```
LTC Francis B. Burns
Unit # 43213
1CD MTT
APO, AE 09344
```

Will try to get mail, baggage from up north that has been sent to me.

   Sorting through the new job, staff organization, etc. Trying to get organized, looking at systems, what works, and what doesn't.

   Also, trying to look at the team that was assembled here. Most of them are from Ft Bliss, and haven't worked together before.

*All*

*Will try to send something out 1x week to all. It's SUN a.m. here, as we're 8 hrs. ahead of EST.*

* * *

Below is the last email sent from my first tour in Iraq. In that I had spent well over a year in theater, you can see that I had a little more on my mind as I was slated to go home soon. I am not quite sure that the random thoughts made any connection to anything in particular. Nonetheless, the ambassadorship of the tour was coming to its end.

```
20 JAN 08
```

```
I first embraced this poem in 1995, and Don
```

Rutherford, who served as our coach, (or "The Don," as he was affectionately known by members of The Frankfurt American Rugby Club, or FARCers) used this poem to encourage a bunch of rugby players to return to Scotland and England, one more time. We were playing in a tournament in Washington, DC, that served as a reunion of sorts. As I was just 31 years old at the time, I don't think the words initially hit home as much as they should have. Now, as the years have passed since that tournament as well as the reunion tour in Scotland and England actually occurring and being part of it, the poem means so much more to me. It is not only the words and their meaning, but from whom delivered them.

## Back Azimuths

*Ulysses, by Alfred Tennyson*

*It profits not that an idle king...*

*I am part of all that I have met;*
*Yet all experience is an arch where thro'*
*Gleams that untravell'd world who margin fades*
*Forever and forever when I move.*
*How dull it is to pause, to make an end,*
*To rust unburnish'd, not to shine in use!*

*Tho' much is taken, much abides; and tho'*
*We are not now that strength which in old days*
*Moved earth and heaven, that which we are, we are;*
*One equal temper of heroic hearts,*
*Made weak by time and fate, but strong in will*
*To strive, to seek, to find, and not to yield*

```
All the best.
GO PATS!
R/
FB
```

\* \* \*

Below is the first of the weekly emails sent during my deployment from 2011-12 for Operation New Dawn. Upfront, in addition to the term back azimuth, there is a tip of the hat to Pete Blaber's book, *Mission, Men, and Me*. The line of Iraqi government having to make a formal request for US to act was prescient, in that as US and NATO withdrew its combat forces, there remained about 125 or so still in Iraq and our fate was uncertain as December 21, 2011, approached.

```
All,                                    7 AUG 11

Back in Iraq. Arrived here on 29 July. Be-
lieve I am perhaps shooting the proverbi-
al back azimuth too much by comparison to
the last time here in respect to the overall
condition of Iraq, the mission, people, and
me—job, living, and working conditions, etc.
Or, maybe it's the new guy syndrome. Also,
being new, I have seen / experienced the five
types of power: Expert, Reward, Legitimate,
Referent, and Coercive. It's acronym haven,
so have had to adjust / adapt. With new ideas
/ concepts, three steps: saturate, incubate,
illuminate. Unsure if I'll get to the illumi-
nate part for a while.
   Have tried to settle in routine, as crea-
ture comforts have tremendously improved: Able
to attend Mass Tue evening, sleep on a firm
mattress, have own bathroom, gym is open 24/7,
have great dining facility, a small barber-
shop, and a post exchange (PX). Definitely miss
being with the family most of all—the hardest
part of deployment is indeed the separation. I
believe that the best place to find yourself is
in a combat (zone) or in jail.
   Three messages here: (1) [Are] Iraqi Se-
curity Forces able to provide internal and
```

external security; (2) [Does the] US has [ve] an enduring partnership, and (3) [Is] Iraq integrated into the region—economically, diplomatically, and security-wise. There are news reports of Iraq wanting to purchase additional F-16s. Also, as 31 December draws closer, Iraq is wanting more US trainers to remain. The Iraqi government must make a formal request for the US to act. There's still a lot of Iranian influence here. I'll leave it at that.

They are definitely in a tougher, more kinetic fight in Afghanistan, though, as a CH-47 cargo helicopter was brought down, and 31 Killed In Action (KIA). Thoughts and prayers go out to them, their families, and units.

Feel as if I have done my time in Purgatory after having been here previously and having been stationed at both The Pentagon and at Fort Polk.

Will try to compose these SUN mornings as I settle into a routine.

Best to all.
R/
FB

\*\*\*

This is the last weekly email sent from Iraq. Although it discusses "liberty without wisdom," perhaps it is a bit more stoic in its tone, and thankful for the support through the deployment.

```
Good Morning,                          15 JUL 12

This week a couple of quotes come to mind.
    First, from James Baldwin, who was a lec-
turer in a class I took at U-Mass @ Am-
herst. "Not everything that is faced may be
changed, but nothing can be changed until it
is faced."⁵³
    I believe that Iraq needs to look at itself
internally to solve its problems, in order to
be a better democracy.
    Another quote is from Edmund Burke, a Brit-
ish Statesman and Philosopher. Although he
may be better known by, "All that is neces-
sary for the triumph of evil is for good men
to do nothing," the following, which is in
reference to 14 July 1789, and the French
Revolution, is also very applicable to pres-
ent day Iraq, which had its own revolution on
14 July 1958, when a secret military group
known as the free officers, overthrew the mon-
arch and killed King Faisal II: "But what is
liberty without wisdom, and without virtue?
It is the greatest of all possible evils; for
```

---

53. James Baldwin quote. Retrieved February 1, 2022 from https://www.goodreads.com/quotes/14374-not-everything-that-is-faced-can-be-changed-but-nothing.

it is folly, vice, and madness, without tuition or restraints."[54]

There are certainly some struggles internal to Iraq, and at times it seems that they we have indeed given them "liberty without wisdom."

Darlene—with Chip & Kelly Chase's assistance (the newlyweds, who live in DC)—is still looking for a house for us. There are more homes now available with the time frame in which we will be there, so things are looking up.

With my replacement here and assuming my duties, I'm scheduled to begin the trek, or duffle bag drag (DBD), from here through Kuwait, back home this week.

A recently arrived priest this week compared deployments to life's journey, with all of us looking forward to the final date but remaining industrious [in the proper manner and towards each other] in the time-between. He was hinting about how we live our dash…the time between our birth date and death. Please remember the 4,487 US Service members whose "dash" includes them giving the ultimate sacrifice here.

Thank for your continued support this past year.

---

54. Edmund Burke quote. Retrieved February 1, 2022 from https://www.goodreads.com/quotes/70711-but-what-is-liberty-without-wisdom-and-without-virtue-it.

## Francis B. Burns

All the best.
R/
FB
FRANCIS B. BURNS
COL, USA
J3, OSC-I
SVOIP:
NPR:
TANDBERG:

## Personal Reflection

- In writing those weekly emails while deployed, I attempted to make a connection on where I was (literally) and figuratively (in what was going on in my mind during the deployment(s))
- Similar to many service members, I have filled many a Green Notebook based upon my experiences. A green notebook is a 5" x 8" green hard-covered memorandum book. Related to this, I regularly listen to Joe Byerly's podcast, *From the Green Notebook*, which is done extremely well, and offers additional reflection on different leader's thoughts from a green notebook.

## Contemplate

How am I living my dash?

What are my priorities?

How do I express my priorities?

# Fellowship

Out of a friendly feeling.

**Insight:** Acts of the Apostles 2:42.

*"They devoted themselves to the teaching of the apostles and to the communal life, to the breaking of bread and to the prayers."*

The Greek word for thanksgiving is *eucharistia*. Its origin is from early Christians and linked the celebration of Christ's last supper with thanksgiving. My brother Michael alluded to this in the summer of 2016, as our family and friends gathered in fellowship to celebrate my mother's 90th birthday.

**Inspire:** I have always enjoyed the film, *It's A Wonderful Life*, starring Jimmy Stewart as George Bailey, who, who after wishing he'd had never been born is visited by an angel, Clarence. Clarence shows George what life would be like in the town of Bedford Falls if that were true. During the flashback of his life, George and his wife Mary bring a housewarming gift to the Martini family consisting of bread, salt, and wine, and use the following,

*Bread, that this house may never know hunger.*
*Salt, that life may always have flavor.*
*And wine, that joy and prosperity may reign forever.* [55]

Also, being a cradle Catholic, a rendition of the Leonardo da Vinci's The Last Supper, is hung in the dining room of many homes. It certainly was in our family when we were growing up, and we always have one hanging in our dining area.

**Ignite:** Sharing and Thanksgiving.

*Thanksgiving Day, 2007, Baghdad, Iraq.*

While growing up in a family of eight other siblings, we had a menu of meals by days of the week, and featured a meat, starch, and vegetable, followed by dessert. Yes, there also was plenty of

---

55. 52 Little Lessons from It's a Wonderful Life.

milk, as we used to have milk, in glass bottles, delivered to us from Harper Farms.

**Sunday:** large meal at 12:30 p.m.—some sort of roast with a vegetable and mashed potatoes (think Seamus Heaney's *When All The Others Were Away At Mass*) [56]

**Monday:** leftovers ground in a fricassee over, you guessed it, mashed potatoes

**Tuesday:** meatloaf and baked potato

**Wednesday:** pasta with meatballs (not meat sauce)

**Thursday:** chicken or pork chops or steak or liver

**Friday:** fish: broiled, baked, fish sticks, smelts, etc.

---

56. *When All The Others Were Away At Mass*, Seamus Haney. Retrieved December 1, 2021 from https://fsgworkinprogress.com. Our son Cormac, sent me this poem after my mother's funeral. I still carry it with me:

When all the others were away at Mass
I was all hers as we peeled potatoes.
They broke the silence, let fall one by one
Like solder weeping off the soldering iron:
Cold comforts set between us, things to share
Gleaming in a bucket of clean water.
And again let fall. Little pleasant splashes
From each other's work would bring us to our senses.

So while the parish priest at her bedside
Went hammer and tongs at the prayers for the dying
And some were responding and some crying
I remembered her head bent towards my head,
Her breath in mine, our fluent dipping knives –
Never closer the whole rest of our lives.

**Saturday:** noon—hotdogs, evening—hamburgers.

We always looked forward to celebrating Thanksgiving with family. Thanksgiving is about sharing what you have with others. It's about them. It is giving that we receive.

Following on the theme of sharing weekly emails while deployed, below are some thoughts that I had during the Thanksgivings spent in Iraq in 2006—2007, and 2011. No one likes to be away from home. The military have fought and continue to fight in the 'Away' games, so that we do not have to.

```
26 NOV 06
Classification: UNCLASSIFIED
All Concerned (ALCON),
```

Trust all had a Happy Thanksgiving? Really took care of us over here—had prime rib, turkey, salmon, shrimp, mashed potatoes, stuffing gravy, many veggies, salad, and of course choice of pies—pumpkin, pecan, apple. Very well done with decorations, etc. Everyone got an opportunity to get a little time to enjoy the holiday.

  [It's] Not as bad as portrayed in the news, although it could certainly get worse. Mosques were not burned to the ground, although one was set on fire, [there was] mostly smoke damage inside. People were not burned as reported via the media. What is correct on the news, is that the curfew still is in effect. Some are comparing recent attacks in

## Back Azimuths

Sadr City to the Samara Mosque bombing. It remains very sectarian, with the Shia militia retaliating for attacks in Sadr City. Will see what meetings next week bring w/ President G.W. Bush & Prime Minister Malaki. Difficult to convince some folks about democracy and what it brings—they were suppressed for so long, all they know is dictatorship, and that way of life.

[There is] Similarity to comparing this to Vietnam and the loss of public support, again due to a certain party withdrawing $$ for that government. Patience is not our forte. Kind of ironic that the word for yes in Arabic is "Nam."

All the best.
R/
FB

25 NOV 07

All,

Two great holidays this month—Veterans Day and Thanksgiving. Hope that all had a great Thanksgiving. Mine was quite memorable. I was enroute back from Kuwait, and my MiTT (Military Transition Team) duties, and had an overnight layover at Victory Base. I was fortunate to go out and visit troops from my brigade at some remote outposts with Lieutenant Colonel Kurt Pinkerton's battalion. They are truly out there amongst the population winning hearts and minds in Abu Ghraib and the vicinity. Soldiers were taking a break—playing flag football, having a Texas Hold 'Em Tournament, cooking turkeys over a skewer (had six each, they cooked them all), and enjoying reprieve from the daily grind. It was just good to go out and shake Soldiers' hands and say Happy Thanksgiving to them. I was surprised to return to the MiTT base and see the attached signs that the Iraqi Soldiers had made for us. The MiTT was able to get plenty of food, dessert, as no one was hungry that day. A very good spread for all to enjoy.

R/
FB

This is another Thanksgiving message from Operation New Dawn. As I am reading it again, in addition to giving thanks, I also provided some insight into the ongoings in theater. Lastly, I closed it out with a quote from the beginning of Anton Myrer's *Once An Eagle*.

Good Morning,                              27 NOV 11

Happy belated Thanksgiving to all! I was very fortunate in that I was able to Skype with my mother and family who were celebrating Thanksgiving at my sister Melanie and brother-in-law Paul Harris' Bed & Breakfast, The Snow Squall Inn, in Wiscasset, ME. It was wonderful to see and speak to them. Darlene and the kids travelled to Texas, where we had attended family Christian camp (Pine Cove) this past summer. They served dinner at 7 p.m. on Thursday and spent a few days there.

 We were once again well taken care of here—turkey, prime rib, lobster tails, pie. We had no scheduled activities, but still meetings, email, etc. So, we got some down time. Below is an interesting article on number of Turkeys over the years sent here and to Afghanistan.

## Battleland.Blogs.Time.com, *Warbirds: Dark Or Light?* By Mark Thompson

There is a rough correlation between the number of U.S. troops fighting in Afghanistan and Iraq, and the number of turkeys sent there annually to help them celebrate Thanksgiving. Your Battleland math whiz has stuffed data provided by the Defense Logistics Agency's troop support folks into his abacus to generate this chart and can safely report: the number of whole turkeys in-bound to the war zones has fallen 57% since 2009.

Over the same two years, the number of U.S. troops in both theaters has dropped from about 175,000 to 115,000. That's a decline of

```
only 34%. This is good news for the troops:
even as your numbers decline, more of you
will be getting drumsticks.
   Number of Turkeys Delivered to Afghanistan
and Iraq:
```

- 2008: 12,419
- 2009: 13,710
- 2010: 7,060
- 2011: 5,863

Speaking of Turkey: Even though negotiations about our Security Agreements are ongoing, PM Malaki is headed to Japan. "Although Turkey and many GCC nations prohibit Iraqi commercial airliners from landing at their airports because of disputes over debts, the Japanese not only forgave Iraq's sovereign debt but also underwrote a huge loan for infrastructure development."

And, here's another turkey, who is currently in US custody:

*Wall Street Journal*, U.S. Clashes With Baghdad Over Fate Of Last Detainee, By Julian E. Barnes and Evan Perez

The case also marks the latest wrinkle in President Barack Obama's efforts to deal with detainees—and could lead to the first military commission proceedings on U.S. soil since World War II. Mr. Obama has collided with political resistance to plans for closing the U.S. detention center in Guantanamo Bay, Cuba, and for prosecuting terrorism suspects in civilian courts.

   Ali Mussa Daqduq, a Lebanese Hezbollah commander accused by

the U.S. of orchestrating the 2007 kidnapping and murder of five U.S. soldiers, is the last remaining detainee in Iraq in American custody.

- His name reminds me of Star Wars character, Count Daku. We should have shipped him to Guantanamo Bay after we arrested him.—FBB

20 NOV 11, Sot Al-Iraq—Iraq will grant partial immunity to US trainers

A government source revealed Sunday that the government is leaning toward granting a partial immunity to U.S. trainers. He revealed Iraq's need for 750 trainers.

The source told al-Mustakbal News Agency, "The government is seriously considering to find a legal and diplomatic solution to grant a partial immunity to foreign trainers who will work on training Iraqi forces after the U.S. withdrawal by the end of 2011."

He added, "Several options are being considered currently, most importantly the granting of partial immunity to U.S. trainers in the event they remain in Iraq." He explained that the government recognizes the need of approximately 750 trainers in the field of Air Force, counter-terrorism, and training on modern machines imported for the Iraqi security forces."

"Indications of some movement within the government on legal protections. Unfortunately, having it leaked to Iraqi media means there is significant opposition within the government to the idea, and this is a cheap way to mobilize opposition and send a message to the PM".—FBB

```
Just when you think that things are going
well...
    The Council of Representatives will vote on
```

```
Thursday on a proposal refusing the extension
of any U.S. Forces in Iraq post-2011.
```

"We have not seen anything on this topic before and am not sure what the implications might be if passed. Assume it is more a "sense of the Congress" than a binding resolution without the PM's approval, but will defer to judgment of others with better knowledge of the Iraqi government. Obviously, if the worst case applies, this could degrade our ability to perform our mission."

*Wall Street Journal*, U.S. Cautions Iraq to Curb Iran Forays, By Sam Dagher

BAGHDAD—Weeks before the withdrawal of U.S. forces from Iraq, the commander of American forces here urged the Iraqi government to keep fighting extremists, and especially the Iran-backed militias he said threaten to form a state within a state.

The commander, Gen. Lloyd Austin, compared the threat to Hezbollah, the Shiite military and political group in Lebanon that has strong ties to Iran and Syria and that the U.S. deems a terrorist group.

"These are elements that are really focused on creating a Lebanese Hezbollah kind of organization in this country: a government within a government," he said. "As we leave, if these elements are left unchecked, they will then eventually turn on the government."

"This is clearly not an endpoint," he said. "We really intend to remain engaged with Iraq, and we look forward to having Iraq as a great strategic partner in the future."

```
This is indeed a very unique way to end a
war. Although viewed as War Termination, it
may be more a War Transition.
```

## Back Azimuths

In reference to Iraq exercising its sovereignty, I am reminded that what we are experiencing now is similar to the opening Aeschylus quote of Anton Myrer's classic,

*"Once an Eagle"*

So in the Libyan fable it is told
That once an eagle, stricken with a dart,
Said, when he saw the fashion of the shaft,
"With our own feathers, not by others' hands,
Are we now smitten." [57]

All the best.
R/
FB

---

[57]. Once An Eagle, Anton Myrer. Introduction.

Francis B. Burns

## Personal Reflection

- Thanksgiving is about sharing what you have with others. It's about them. It is giving that we receive.
- It was and still is heartwarming to see that the military recognizes the importance of fellowship and makes Thanksgiving, Christmas, and other holidays special for service members.

Back Azimuths

## Contemplate

What's the best meal story or fellowship that you have shared?
_____
_____
_____
_____
_____

What are the special memories about that meal?
_____
_____
_____
_____
_____

What Thanksgiving traditions do you celebrate? What traditions have you in turn passed to your children or to the next generation?
_____
_____
_____
_____
_____

# Sponsorship

One who enters into an engagement, makes a formal promise or pledge on behalf of another.

**Insight:** Matthew 7:12.

*"Do to others whatever you would have them do to you." The Golden Rule*

Being the new guy /gal or part of a new family or organization, we often feel as if we were being judged—hint, hint, we are. Although Ted Lasso is fond of quoting Walt Whitman's, "Be curious, not judgmental,"[58] it is difficult to just to be curious in the Army, as I sense that there tended to be a sense of competition vs. completion when one moves from duty station to station. Nonetheless, there should always be a proper welcoming of a new face / arrival / team member / co-worker.

---

58. Sudeikis, Jason. Ted Lasso. Apple TV+. 2020. Season 1, Episode 8. Misquoting Walt Whitman. Retrieved February 2, 2022 from https://poppoetry.substack.com/p/ted-lasso-misquotes-walt-whitman. "*Be curious, not judgmental* is excellent advice. It sounds like Whitman, and it contains a certain democratic, Whitmanic generosity of spirit. But the only nod to curiosity in Whitman's well-known *Leaves of Grass* is the phrase "Be not curious about God."

**Inspire:** My initial tenure at Fort Polk, Louisiana in 2008 was similar to the reception received by George W. Bush during his initial elected tenure as a politician in Texas, "Why do we have to listen to a Yankee educated fella to come here to tell us what to do?"

At other locations or positions that I have held, I have heard the sentiment of, "Who does he / she think he / she is? We're not a military unit. He just can't order us to do something."

Still, upon arrival at other locations, I was warmly greeted, the office was cleaned, desks empty, the computer was set-up, the in-processing checklist ready to go, and necessary appointments were scheduled. So, proper welcoming can and does occur, and when it does, the sense of welcoming and belonging are felt in a positive way.

People may not remember your name, but you will never forget how they made you feel. Wherever we are, we need to ensure a proper onboarding to new folks.

**Ignite:** Welcoming.

*U-Haul truk and car trailer, similar to one described in this chapter.*

Dependent upon the position, there are both hard and soft skills that are emphasized during arrival of a new employee. I can remember when I was young Company Commander (Captain) at Fort Drum, NY in Company A, 2nd Battalion, 22nd Infantry Regiment, and the welcoming way mirrored what the 75th Ranger Regiment then emphasized: marksmanship, physical training, medical / 1st Aid training, and small unit tactics. At that time, and at that level, there was not much focus on the use of soft skills.

A proper sense of welcoming that one feels when one arrives to a new location / job / unit / organization was evident when I worked for Lieutenant General Mike Ferriter (US Army, Retired). His three thoughts on welcoming others were based on: (1) Do your best (2) Be hard and (3) Be dependable.

When I or others went to work for him, there was never a trial period or having to prove oneself. One was immediately accepted and acknowledged for what he / she brought to the unit. Whether it was incoming personnel, or just passing by folks (this made it challenging while in the Pentagon and going from meeting to meeting) his saying was, "It doesn't cost a penny to make someone feel like a million dollars." To this day, he continues to be very engaging and positive in demeanor.

While giving talks, Lieutenant General Ferriter often related a story on sponsorship of which he was part of after he and his travel party checked in to an on-post hotel. A large U-Haul moving truck with a car on a trailer in tow was trying to back into a parking space. He and his Command Sergeant Major Earl Rice and his enlisted aide, Master Sergeant Tohonn Nicholson approached the vehicle. Upon approach, a very distraught woman, who was an Army spouse, rolled down the window and stated she was having a hard time backing up the truck. Master Sergeant Nicholson said, "No worries, I got this," and jumped into the cab of the truck after she got out. Master Sergeant Nicholson then quickly jumped out of the cab of the truck and said, "There's a German shepherd in the passenger seat." The spouse went to the other side of the U-Haul moving truck and got the dog out. Master Sergeant Nicholson then re-entered the cab of the truck, and, under the ground guidance of Command Sergeant Major Rice was able to park the vehicle and ensure all was secure.

Lt Gen Ferriter and Command Sergeant Major Rice then asked where she was coming from, and more importantly, who was her sponsor? They took the time to ensure that the sponsor met up with the spouse, whose husband was deployed, and ensure she was checked into the hotel and settled. Although, it seems as if it is a small act, recognizing that one is in need and doing something about it went a long way in establishing a better welcome to the installation then when the spouse first pulled into the parking lot after having driven a long distance, with a pet, hauling a moving trailer with a car in tow, to a new location.

## Personal Reflection

- I have tried to follow Lieutenant General Ferriter's lead and develop my own mantra when meeting and greeting new personnel. There should be an acceptance for who you are, no matter the circumstance. It is important upfront, when meeting new personnel to ensure a proper welcome.
- In my current role, I meet with all new employees and share with them what I value, which is:

>Listening to Understand
>Building Trust
>Developing Relationships
>Humility
>Gratitude

## Contemplate

What is the best way to accept others for who they are?

_____
_____
_____
_____
_____

Describe your best or worst welcoming to an organization?

_____
_____
_____
_____
_____

What will you change in how you welcome people to your Family / organization?

_____
_____
_____
_____
_____

# Mentorship

The proper name of Mentor, person with whom Telemachus' upbringing was left; when Odysseus was away at war; experienced and trusted counselor.

**Insight:** 1 Thessalonians 5:11.

*"Therefore, encourage each other and build one another up, as indeed you do."*

I previously wrote of the Friday afternoons spent at Fort Benning when I encountered Brigadier General Yarbrough in the field with the Drill Sergeants and new Soldiers. At that time I served as a Commander of a One Station Unit Training (OSUT) Battalion, consisting of six companies, and cadre of Drill Sergeants. The Drill Sergeants serve as mentors and try to be hard on the standard, not on the Soldier. Many of us still remember our Drill Sergeants / Drill Instructors / First coach / First leader / First mentor and what they mean to us. You never know when or where your influence may end or begin.

**Inspire:** To whom to we entrust others, our sons and daughters? Teachers? Coaches? Neighbors? Babysitters? Family members? Friends? Relatives? Do we entrust our sons and daughters to a Scout Master, Merit Badge Counselor, Youth Coach, teacher, musical instrument teacher? Telemachus, the son of Odysseus, was taught by Mentor when Odysseus was away at war.

During time spent in the military and especially during deployments, we are not always able to be there for certain life events. So, similar to Odysseus prior to the Trojan War, when we are away, we entrust the upbringing of our own kin to others.

**Ignite:** Pay it forward.

*Telemachus and Mentor.* [59]

I started the practice of writing a letter to certain high school seniors a few years ago. This was when our youngest was a senior at St. John Paul II (SJPII) Catholic High School in Schertz, TX. Unfortunately, I had anticipated the team advancing further into

---
59. Telemachus and Mentor. Retrieved February 2, 2022 from http://ulyssesetc.blogspot.com/2013/04/stephen-and-telemachus.html.

the playoffs and had to write the letters following their final game vice prior to their playoff run. In 2021 and again 2022, I wrote similar letters to the current SJPII Senior Soccer Players. In the letter, I hoped to plant a seed as they entered the playoffs of their final high school sports season.

*February 11, 2021*

*Ms. Adrianna Shuck*
*Saint John Paul II Catholic High School*
*6720 FM 482*
*New Braunfels, TX 78132*

*Dear Adrianna,*

*"No one knows the day or the hour."—Matthew 24:36*

*Often times we do not have the courtesy to know when the 'last' of some things come. I wanted to write something to you as you start the playoff run.*

*Thank you for allowing me to live vicariously through you these past few years. It has been incredible to experience on my end—the passion, the determination, the fierceness, the camaraderie; yet, you have lived it.*

*As you know, sometimes sports, or a specific sport like soccer, can seem like the entire world in high school, and sports is often viewed as a metaphor for life.*

*You should be beyond proud of who you are, your teammates, all who supported you—your family, your coaches, your school—all that you represent, and, all of what you've accomplished.*

*When you remember your high school soccer career, don't think of one game. Instead, reflect back on all of the wins, the road trips, the laughter, the practices, the cold January nights, the team dinners, the bruises, pulls, and sprains, the drills, the off-season workouts, the discipline, the motivational quotes, the seemingly endless grind of it all, and the teammates. There is so much to appreciate now, and more so in the years that follow.*

*Take the many lessons learned on the fields of friendly strife with you and let them positively shape you on your journey. "I am a part of all that I have met..." — Ulysses, Tennyson*

*You represent all that is good about high school athletics. You have had a significant impact on the soccer pitch, the SJPII campus, and the community.*

*So, in this year of 'lasts' for you, allow me to be the 'first' to say that I am I am proud of you and the woman that you all have become.*

*Keep the attack going, maintain faith in yourself, and in God.*

*Nolite Timere!*

*Francis B. Burns*
*Colonel, U.S. Army (Retired)*

There are many mentors who have had a positive impact on me. At the time, the person may not have realized their impact. I have attempted to capture some of the many mentors with whom I have had the fortune to be associated. There are many more, those whom I served with in the military, in the education field, and now in the Department of the Army Civilian Work Force.

## Examples of Mentorship While Growing Up

Fr. Richard Hannigan. Catholic Priest. USMC Chaplain, Vietnam Veteran. After having served for 20+ years, chose to come back to be at his high school alma mater and be a part of our lives.

Mr. Walter A. Carew, Jr., aka Coach Carew. High school English Teacher. A WW II Infantry Captain, who was called back for the Korean War. After having served during both WW II and then being called back to service for the Korean War, he chose to pay it forward by being a coach. After having retired from teaching and coaching, he briefly sold insurance, then saw an opening in the classified section that a small Catholic high school in Fitchburg, Massachusetts was searching for a teacher and head football coach. He was the youngest of a family of 12, and he and his wife Catherine had five children. He is a member of the Massachusetts Coaching Hall of Fame in both football and baseball. When our middle son was playing football at Paul VI Catholic High School in Fairfax, VA, the offensive line coach was also from Massachusetts, and remembered him fondly.

Mr. Anthony (Tony) Cataldi. Another WW II Veteran, having served in the Navy Construction Battalion (SeaBees). My brother Rick's father-in-law, is from whom I learned about tearing down and re-building homes and all that it entails. The best compliment that he gave was, "That's a good piece of labor."

Sr. Mary Virginia, Presentation of the Blessed Virgin Mary (PBVM). She received a PhD from Boston University and was a Latin Teacher at St. Bernard's Central Catholic High School, Fitchburg, MA. On the first day of Latin class my freshmen year, she wrote a sentence on the blackboard using 5 cases and a 1st conjugation verb. She broke the sentence down and explained to us that this is the how and what we would be learning our freshmen year. She continued to write to me during my 1st tour in Iraq, with perfect Palmer—Method handwriting.

Lieutenant Colonel Robert Grudziecki, US Air Force Reserve, Retired. He is another High school teacher, this one in Social Studies. He also served as an assistant football coach and Track & Field Coach. He continued to show us what it was like to be a citizen-soldier, make a subject relatable, and maintain a sense of humor. In addition to his assistance in getting me into ROTC at the University of Massachusetts at Amherst, he was the driving force to get me to come from Louisiana to Massachusetts to speak at the Leominster WW II and Korean Monument Dedication Ceremony.

Fr. Barry Bercier, Augustinians of Assumption (A.A), Catholic Priest. He was also high school teacher of Literature at St. Bernard's. He read and brought to life Homer's *Iliad* & *Odyssey*, Vergil's *Aeneid*, Dante's *Inferno*, *Beowulf*, and Shakespeare's *Julius Caesar*. He was a lay teacher at St. Bernard's, and left to become an Assumptionist Priest. In addition to his spiritual example and guidance, I credit him with instilling in me the appreciation of literature and all that it entails.

## Examples of Peer Mentorship
## Vetrepeneurs (of sorts)

Bob "Java Bob" Garver. US Army Veteran. In the early 1990s, he used some of the money he received when the Army downsized to buy a coffee roaster and start a coffee company in Santa Cruz, CA, named Java Bob's. After having established a flourishing business on the west coast in 10 years, he sold it all and picked up and re-started an organic coffee company in Brunswick, ME, called Wicked Joe. He possesses incredible business acumen, has a wonderful family, is and has recently branched out to Wicked Tea.

Rob "Brisket" Harris. USMC Veteran, Semper Fi. We met when he was a 17-year-old high school student in Wiesbaden, (then) Federal Republic of Germany, and the brother of "Tall Paul" Harris, a fellow rugby player, and now a Professor at Auburn University. Rob was a 1 800 GOT JUNK franchise owner in Atlanta. He is an extremely hard worker, and through his grit has become quite the businessman.

Bob "Ando" Anderson. US Army Veteran. Bob was an integral part of the Panama Invasion. After getting out of the Army, he led Stevenson Prep School in Pebble Beach, CA, and also coached football and lacrosse. He is a great family and Christian man, and Founder of Leading Challenges, 1 Hero Sports, and a mentor to me on Emotional Intelligence.

Paul "Devo" Devereaux. US Army Veteran. Paul worked in the medical device field and served as a Senior Vice President of a large medical company. Another incredible family man and is able to use some skills garnered from the military to excel in the business world and coaching youth lacrosse.

Daniel Richard. Major, Massachusetts State Police. I think most folks have a childhood friend that they can reach back to at any time, and conversation picks up from where it last was. Dan'l enlisted in the Army out of high school (along with five others from our high school), jumped into Grenada, received an ROTC commission as I swore him into the Army, served his time as a Military Police Corps, became a local policeman, became a state trooper, K9 specialist, Detective, and made his way through the ranks to Major. Oh, he is an NCAA Division I Football official, serving in the Big 10. He possesses exceptional character and is part of a great Christian family.

## Examples of Higher Level Worker Mentorship

Jan Mening. In the spring of 2001, I had no idea what rank a Senior Executive Service (SES) was when I first spoke with Ms. Mening about a possible position working as her Executive Officer in the Pentagon. Upon arrival at The Pentagon, I found out that she was the equivalent of a 3-Star General, and certainly carried the professionalism, as well as the clout. Through her presence and knowledge, I experienced firsthand the meaning of Department of the Army Civilians are the conduit in which the Army runs, and the necessity of the civilian oversight of the military.

Pat Flynt. Pat is extremely knowledgeable and professional is every sense of those words. She served as a teacher and mentor for me in the installation management field, as I was a young officer trying to find out my role in the Pentagon, while assigned to the Base Realignment and Closure Office, as well as in the Army.

Diane Randon. I worked indirectly for Ms. Randon during my second tour at The Pentagon. Another SES, who exemplified in word and action professionalism in every sense of the word. She currently serves in the Pentagon as the Deputy to the Department of the Army G2, Intelligence.

Earl Rice, Command Sergeant Major, US Army, Retired. CSM Rice and I served together in the Pentagon and spent many hours working and traveling together. He is smart, articulate, physically fit, a strong Christian with a wonderful family. It was not until his retirement that I realized he was a Native American.

Cheryl Kearney, Brigadier General, US Air Force, Retired. Brig Gen Kearney was serving as a Political Science Professor at the United States Air Force Academy when she volunteered to serve in Iraq as a Political Military Advisor. She possesses a keen mind and was a great Christian friend while in Baghdad. She recently retired to Pennsylvania with her family.

Paul "Tall Paul" Harris, PhD, Professor, Department Head, Political Science, Auburn University. Another longtime friend from my time in the then Federal Republic of Germany. Tall Paul is smart, articulate, funny and is able to relate well to all with whom he meets.

Mike Ferriter, Lieutenant General, US Army, Retired. LTG (Ret) Ferriter is the epitome of positive leadership and thinking. Our paths initially crossed from 1999-2001 at Fort Benning, Georgia when he assumed command of the 11th Infantry Regiment. Although he had served most of his career in the 75th Ranger Regiment, he now was on the Training and Doctrine (TRADOC) side of the Army. Using the Abrams Charter foundation of Rangers who served in the Rangers going out and setting a personal example of excellence wherever they may be, he approached the position in a way that it doesn't matter the card which you are dealt. For example, he was instrumental in bringing the Modern Army Combatives Program into the Regular Army through the enlisted, non-commissioned officer, and officer training base at Fort Benning. I next served with him in Iraq in 2011, and then at The Pentagon. He is another incredible family man, and he hosted my retirement ceremony. He possesses an extremely exemplary demeanor, and currently serves as the Director of the National Veterans Museum and Memorial (NVMM) in Columbus, Ohio.

Bob Caslen, Lieutenant General, US Army, Retired. I served as LTG (Ret) Caslen's joint operations officer in Baghdad from 2011-2012. After the withdrawal of US combat forces from Iraq in December 2011, we were left with 126 military personnel, a few thousand contractors, and no security agreement. In 2011 in Baghdad, Iraq, he stated that this had taken all his (then) 37 years of experience to work his way through this — How can we partner in a country and at the same time go to war with a country that we are not at war with? He later served as Superintendent at United States Military Academy (USMA) as well as President at The University of South Carolina.

## Personal Reflection

- Always attempt to pay it forward.
- Give back to others.
- We do not always know if the seed has been planted, or, if it is planted amongst weeds.

Francis B. Burns

## Contemplate

Who serve or have served as the mentors in your life?

_____
_____
_____
_____
_____

In lieu of actually being there every day, is there someone who offers their service to those whom you love?

_____
_____
_____
_____
_____

To whom can I serve as a mentor?

_____
_____
_____
_____
_____

# Scholarship

Learning, erudition; especially proficiency in the Greek
and Latin languages and their literature.

**Insight:** Psalms 32:8.

*"I will instruct you and show you the way you should walk, give you counsel with my eye upon you."*

One's educational foundation needs to be established at home. This is done by embracing that parents are the primary educators of children. In addition to the 'how' of learning, parents should be ingrained into the learning process as well.

As previously stated, there are positive and negative qualities that we see and in turn emulate in others. This is especially true in all the...ships, as we learn from those whose example is to be followed or not to be followed.

I appreciate that there are certain things to be memorized which serve as a foundation—math facts, grammar rules, and Latin nouns, phrases, and synopses (that's a personal one). Education stems from the Latin, *e* or *ex* meaning away from, and *duc* meaning to lead. Away from what is one is being led? Ignorance.

**Inspire:** "Education is an ornament in prosperity, refuge in adversity."—Admiral James Stockdale

The above quote on education and scholarship that stands out for me is from Rear Admiral (RADM) James Stockdale. RADM Stockdale was a Prisoner of War in Vietnam for over seven and a half years and received the Medal of Honor. He is remembered as a Stoic, in that he was given a copy of Epictetus' *Enchiridion*, while in graduate school, and carried it with him while deployed. Upon return to the United States, RADM Stockdale served as Commandant of the US Naval War College, as well as President of The Citadel.

From 1994-98, I served at the United States Military Academy Preparatory School (USMAPS) then located at Fort Monmouth, New Jersey. I served as a Tactical Officer, coached football and lacrosse, and then as the school's operations officer. I challenged the 17-21-year-old students, or Prepsters as they are affectionately called, in the following manner, "If at the end of the day, you have not learned anything, you are welcome to knock on my door and we'll learn something together." I did have some take me to task, and often we would open The Compact Oxford English Dictionary and learn something together.

**Ignite:** Lifelong learning.

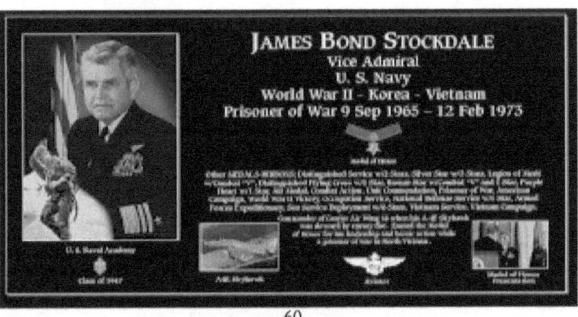

One of my duties while at Fort Polk, Louisiana, was to serve as Graduation Speaker for the colleges that served the base. What I hoped to inspire in the Soldiers and family members was to be a lifelong learner.

\* \* \*

*Welcome and good evening. Thank you for the warm welcome and allowing me to say a few words this evening.*

*It's both an honor and a privilege to speak to you at this graduation ceremony as you move on to the next phase of your lives.*

*With the Christmas trees going up all around us, and our family taking the decorations out of the boxes this past weekend, I was at the same time thinking about what to say tonight, I remembered something that Rear Admiral James Stockdale used quite often when he was a prisoner of war in Vietnam for seven-and-a-half years. It is from Epictetus, "Ed-*

---

60. James Stockdale. Retrieved February 2, 2022 from https://soledadmemorial.org/plaques/medal-honor-recipient-vice-admiral-james-bond-stockdale/.

ucation is an ornament in prosperity and a refuge in adversity."

Spouses, parents, children, family, and friends: thank you for the support given to your graduate.

To the Graduates:

The education has to come first in order to fully appreciate the experience.

Studying and training well is a matter of having the patience to persevere when you are tired and not expecting instant results. The only secret is that it is consistent, often monotonous, boring, hard work. And it's tiring.

Many of you have balanced demanding careers and multiple deployments while achieving educational success. What a monumental task! You've shown that you're not afraid of the sacrifices necessary to make a difference. You've maintained balance in your lives by understanding the concept that character is permanent, and issues are transient.

The most important and most gratifying job anyone can do is passing on one's experience and enthusiasm to the next generation. A teacher affects eternity, he can never tell where his influence stops. Teaching, directly or indirectly, is also the life's work of all those who serve in the armed forces.

So, three points for you tonight: READ, READ, and READ.

In a recent article, General Gordon Sullivan, President of the Association of the United States Army (AUSA) offered the following thoughts on reading:

"Curiosity is the hallmark of a learner, and diligence in application of knowledge is the hallmark of a professional. We have a huge volume of information available to us. Everyone *wants our attention, be it social networking or working out. Reading teaches conceptual analysis, offers insights to ponder, and expands both the imagination and the potential of the mind."*

*He then referred to a letter from Gen Matthew Ridgeway in 1982, which eloquently distilled the riches of lifelong learning:*

*"The formative years of one's life are rich fields for future growth. They pass quickly, but while one has them, they offer boundless opportunities for preparation for the challenges which will surely come.*

*Into those years, even the most privileged can crowd but a few personal experiences, and experience are the great teachers."*

*So, the answer is to draw on the boundless experiences of others. With good fortune you may have opportunities to know men and women of stature—those who have had great experience. Draw directly from them all you can and tuck it away for future use.*

*Such opportunities will be few, but the opportunities to learn of such experiences are unlimited. They lie in the pages of histories, biographies, and the records of those who have gone before you—the records of great successes and great failure of great men and great women, who with the vision to see, the wisdom to choose, and the moral courage to act, reached the heights.*

*So read, read, And READ. The rewards can be great."*

*Where are we today? (Remember this was 2010)*

*Iraq: In 2003, literacy rate below 42%; today close to 76%*

*Afghanistan, where we remain cautiously optimistic:*

*43.6% for men; 12.6% for women; However, only 14% of the Afghan Army can read or write.*

*October 2001 — 600K students in schools, ALL male*
*April 2010 — 6M, of which 60% female*
*I'm not a math guy, but that's something to the tune of 10x increase, isn't it? You see, it's about education over there as well. (N.B. As this was delivered in December 2010, the events of the Afghanistan withdrawal are not taken into consideration).*

*So, you see, your credentials are a vital contribution to your workplace, our communities — and this nation. You have not studied for the sake of studying. It's how you can apply it.*

*You have an awful lot of which to be proud of, yet at the same time, do not let your degree define who you are. If you're not enough without it, you'll never be enough with it.*

*Enjoy and savor this moment, take it all in. Take this experience, with renewed determination, back to your units, your families, and your peers and help improve the lives of those around you — just like you've done for yourselves. The success is complete, the significance begins.*

*Lastly, be sure to hang up your new ornament in a place of significance, so that it will indeed become a refuge in adversity.*

*I congratulate you, their families and friends, and the faculty and administrators upon this occasion. Fort Polk congratulates you. The Army congratulates you. Your credentials are a vital contribution to your workplace, our communities — and this nation.*

*All the best.*
*God Speed.*

## Personal Reflection

- There is always something to learn. Grow every day.
- Leaders are readers. I have a goal to read one book per month. The genres that I read include leadership, biographies, sports, coaching, business, self-help, and historical fiction.
- I believe that there should be a 'learn and live' approach to life, versus a 'live and learn.' Sometimes, we emphasize living vs. learning, or we tend to use experience and failure as a way to set things right. If we learn first, then perhaps the failure would not occur.

Francis B. Burns

## Contemplate

Why do you believe that education is important?

_____
_____
_____
_____
_____

Is education more important than experience? What is the proper blend of education and experience?

_____
_____
_____
_____
_____

What is something that I learned today and shared with others?

_____
_____
_____
_____
_____

# Stewardship

One who manages the affairs of an estate on behalf of his / her employer.

**Insight:** Luke 12:48.

*"Much will be required of the person entrusted with much, and still more will be demanded of the person entrusted with more." A paraphrase of this may be 'Of whom much is given, much is expected.'*

To do well with the gifts given to you requires effort. This Bible verse refers to the word talent, which, is about 20 years' worth of wages for a laborer. If we use $40,000 to $50,000 for a laborer's wage, this is around a $1,000,000 in today's currency. To be able to double the talents is an incredible feat, and the ones who put in the effort and double their talents are rewarded accordingly. The one who buries the talent in the ground, is fearful of losing the talent's worth, or disappoints one who gave them the talent(s). So, the fear, or lack of action, leads to laziness and foolishness. The verse ends with disparagement, the loss of the talent to the one who has the most.

When deciding upon acquisition of a piece of a military piece of equipment, some use the...ilities: Lethality, Adaptability, Sustainability, Disposability, and Capability, amongst others. Perhaps if the one given the one the talent had taken action and used one of the...ilities, the talent would have increased.

**Inspire:** My life is a gift to me from my Creator, what I choose to do with that life is my gift back to Him.—Billy Mills, 1960 5,000 Meter Olympic Gold Medalist.

We all have things to give: time, talent, treasure. As stewards we are entrusted with each. Somehow, these are interwoven into military service. The Greeks used two different words for time, so time can be interpreted as something qualitative such as chronological time or *chronos*, or qualitative time, or *kairos*, which certain moments having a significant meaning. In the same way, both talents can be viewed as that which someone has and uses well, or in the Bible meaning, of wages. Also, treasure can be something we gather here on earth, not necessarily in the next life. Service members, once they depart their respective military service are known as veterans.

The word veteran is used not only to describe those who have served in the military, it is also used to define one who has been with an organization or playing sports for an extended period of time. In trying to understand this, it turns out that the root of the word is actually an adjective. It stems from the Latin, *Vetus, Veteris*, Feminine gender, 3rd Declension, one-termination adjective (non-i-stem).

Adjective: Masculine, Feminine, Neuter
- old, aged, elderly, ancient
- long-standing
- former, previous

Positive: *Vetus, Veteris*
Comparative: *vetustior* or *veterior*
Superlative: *vetustissimus* or *veterrimus*

Perhaps then, we should have different categories for military Veterans? Maybe instead of Veterans' Day, we should rename it Vetustissimus or Veterrimus Day?

**Ignite:** A sense of giving and a sense of duty.

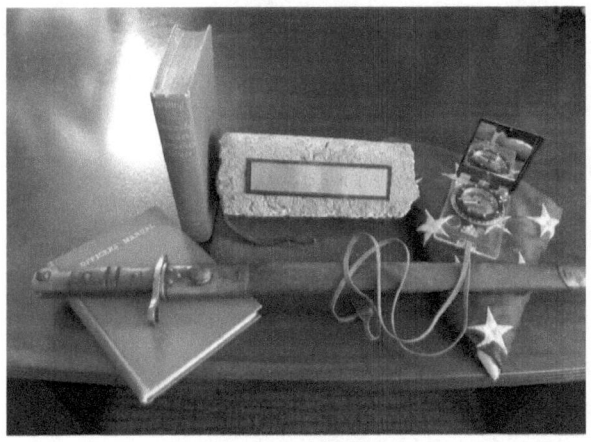

*Items used for Veterans Day Speech: Circa 1918 — Officer's Manual, Rudyard Kipling's Barrack Room Ballads and Departmental Ditties, British Enfield Bayonet; US Flag I carried in my rucksack for many years; chunk of the Berlin Wall from 1989, which I use as a nameplate, and; a Silva Compass.*

From 2016 — 2020, I served as Principal of Our Lady of Perpetual Help (OLPH) Catholic School in Selma, Texas, a K3 — 8th grade school with 400+ students, and 80 or so faculty. Parents who send their children to a Catholic School expect more from the parochial education, as they are actually paying twice — one for property taxes (that fund the public school system), and tuition for their child(ren) to attend Catholic School. Serving as an administrator, staff, or faculty, at any level, is a very demanding job, and I will always respect those who serve in that vocation. In 2019, I used a Veterans Day presentation to attempt to inculcate a sense of duty in the students, faculty, and families.

\* \* \*

*I'm going to give you three numbers, 3, 2, 1. Remember those, alright?*

*It's time for audience participation. After I sing a verse, you just need to sing, "HEY, HEY!" Let's try it.*

*Hey loddi, loddi, "HEY, HEY!"*
*Alright, here we go*

*Hey loddi, loddi, "HEY, HEY!"*
*Hey loddi, loddi, ho "HEY, HEY!"*
*Hey loddi, loddi, "HEY, HEY!"*
*Hey loddi, loddi, ho "HEY, HEY!"*

*Dress it right, and cover down "HEY, HEY!"*
*40 inches all around "HEY, HEY!"*
*Dress it right, and cover down "HEY, HEY!"*
*40 inches all around "HEY, HEY!"*

*Hey loddi, loddi, "HEY, HEY!"*
*Hey loddi, loddi, ho "HEY, HEY!"*
*Hey loddi, loddi, "HEY, HEY!"*
*Hey loddi, loddi, ho "HEY, HEY!"*

## Back Azimuths

*Standing tall, and looking good "HEY, HEY!"*
*Ought to be in Hollywood "HEY, HEY!"*
*Standing tall, and looking good "HEY, HEY!"*
*Ought to be in Hollywood "HEY, HEY!"*

*Hey loddi, loddi, "HEY, HEY!"*
*Hey loddi, loddi, lo "HEY, HEY!"*
*Hey loddi, loddi, "HEY, HEY!"*
*Hey loddi, loddi, lo "HEY, HEY!"*

*Alright, Alright, Alright… Give yourselves a round of applause*

Good afternoon Fr. Frank, Fr. Naveen. Especially welcome the presence of the Our Lady of Perpetual Help (OLPH) military ministry who have joined us this afternoon. (Acknowledge any other VIP present)

I am humbled to be here to assist us in celebrating Veterans Day.

Thank you to Mrs. Nine and the Wildcat Worship Team and thank you to Mrs. Sharp for ensuring that we help celebrate Veterans Day, and for the presentation that we will view in a short while.

And a Happy belated birthday to the United States Marine Corps! Semper Fi and Ooo-Rah!

[Take out my compass and ask,] "What's an azimuth?"

Mr. Taubert and Ms. Victoria Speakmon, Ms. Tackett, Ms. Fleury all wanted me to ensure them that math was worked into the ceremony today. So, on the screen is the definition.

Oh, we can work in science into this, as the magnetic forces of earth are the cause of the compass's arrow, and there is True

*North, magnetic North, Grid North, GM Angle, Left Add Right Subtract...*

*More simply, for us Army folks, it is a direction or a way, mostly used in travel.*

*I have used this compass for thirty couple years and it has assisted me in navigation, both literally and figuratively. I will use it metaphorically today (OK, English gets credit, too) to explain dates and time.*

*In English we have one word for time, time. In Greek, there are two words for time — chronos and kairos.*

*Chronos time is quantitative — How much more time is he going to speak? What time is practice today? Is Christmas still on the 25th of December this year?*

*Kairos time is qualitative — a moment that transcends what we think of as time. Kairos moments don't just occur. We have to put in lots of chronos time — work, study, and effort, sweat, and blood, tears — in order to have kairos moments.*

*I will share three dates with you today, and I will shoot the proverbial back azimuth to help us remember the chronos that makes the Kairos moments happen. Here we go...*

*NOV 7, 2019*

*A great example of a veteran who possessed humility, or Vitamin H, is a man named Rick Rescorla. An Englishman by birth, fought in Rhodesia (Zimbabwe), joined the US Army, is found on the cover of We Were Soldiers Once...And Young, has master's degree in English, law degree, and retired as a Colonel in the US Army. He worked security at the World Trade Center Towers starting in 1991. He sang Cornish hymns in The Battle of Ia Drang Valley, and ensured drills were carried out following 1993 WTC bombings. My favorite quote of his is a few years prior to his death after finding out he had prostate cancer, "I have accepted the fact that there will never be a kairos moment for me, just an uneventful Miltonian plow-the-fields discipline... a few more cups of mocha grande at Starbucks, each one losing a little bit more of its flavor."*[61]

Six days later, on 9/11 he did in fact have another kairos moment, as he is credited in saving close to 2,700 lives at the World Trade Center in NYC. He was awarded the Presidential Citizens Medal on the 7th of November 2019. You see, he was not happy unless he was protecting others.

*NOV 9, 1989*

The US and its allies had been in Europe following WWII and carried out The Marshall Plan. We went through the Berlin Airlift in the years 1948-1949 to ensure that East Germany and USSR would not overtake the city, and a wall was built. NATO had well over 500,000 troops stationed there for over 40 years. Presidents spoke in Berlin — in 1963 President Kennedy offered, "Ich ben ein Berliner"! In 1987 President Reagan demanded, "Mr. Gorbachev, tear down this wall." It did come down a few years later, on November 9, 1989. Many of us were in Germany then to see the jubilation and all that had gone on behind the Iron Curtain for so many years.

[Fall of the Berlin Wall. Show chunk of wall that I have.]

*NOV 11, 1918*

Today we commemorate the 11th day of the 11th hour from 1918, signifying the end of WWI, in order to help us to better

---

61. Rick Rescorla. Retrieved February 9, 2009, from https://www.cmohs.org/citizen-honors/rick-rescorla.

*understand the sacrifice and humility brought out by the service of our Veterans.*

*Some items here from that time period:*
- *British Enfield Bayonet, given to me from friend who fought in Afghanistan. Yes, there is still Cosmoline on its blade. [Show the bayonet]*
- *Rudyard Kipling, author of The Jungle Book, was a war correspondent in India in early 1900s. He wrote the book Barrack Rooms Ballads for the common Soldier, or 'Tommy' as the British Soldier was referred. This was of course before iPhones, Internet, this book was with Soldiers in 1918. [Show the book]*
- *US Officers Manual from 1918—[Show the book]*
- *US Military History book from that time period—[Read some of it]*

*In these examples, and countless others from this one nation under God, Veterans are honest about their weaknesses. They do not ask what do I want from life, rather, they ask themselves what is life asking of me?*

*Today, I shot a back azimuth, gave us some dates and times to remind us that we cannot fight a war without veterans. While the utopian idea of a society without war is appealing, let us not forget that wars have liberated slaves, stopped genocide, and toppled terrorists.*

*OK, that's great, but what can we do? Listen to them, Pray for them.*

*Proverbs 4:7 reads, "The beginning of wisdom is: get wisdom; whatever else you get, get understanding." Or from the prayer of Saint Francis, "… to be understood as to under-*

*stand."⁶² We can gain wisdom by listening to understand them, not to be understood or to respond.*

*Prayer has been a staple of the American experience since the founding of our nation. It's why George Washington "fervently beseech[ed] the Almighty" at Valley Forge and in his farewell address. It's why Abraham Lincoln constantly invoked the name of God in our nation's darkest moments in the Civil War. It's why every session of Congress still opens in prayer.*

*Prayer is a unifying force, especially in a country entrenched in political polarization. It's a way of humbly admitting that as mere humans, we do not have all the answers. Prayer is an expression of hope that someday all the world's evils will come to an end.*

*3, 2, 1: 3 Dates, 2 things we can do for our 1 nation, under God.*

*Our debt to these heroes can never be re-paid, but our gratitude and respect must last forever.*

## Closing

*May God continue to bless our veterans and their families, all those who did not return home, the Prisoners of War, and those missing in action, all veterans, and current members of our armed services, especially those currently deployed and their Families.*

*And may God continue to bless Texas and the United States of America.*

---

62. St. Francis of Assisi: Make Me an Instrument of Your Peace. Retrieved on February 2, 2022 from https://www.archspm.org/faith-and-discipleship/prayer/catholic-prayers/st-francis-of-assisi-make-me-an-instrument-of-your-peace/.

*Amen.*
*Closing Prayer (After Video)*
*Please join with me in reciting the prayer found on the* screens.

## Personal Reflection

- Stewardship, and being entrusted with something of value, is much like mentorship; however, instead of a person who you are looking after, you are entrusted with time, talent, and treasure.
- Have I listened to and prayed for a Veteran today?

## Contemplate

What talents do I have?

How am I using my talents to better myself? My organization?

How can I best develop talent in others? How do I ensure other team member's talents are in synch with each other and the mission and vision of the organization—How do I manage talent?

# Worship

The condition (in a person) of observing or being held in esteem and repute.

**Insight:** John 15:13.

> *"No one has greater love than this, to lay down one's life for one's friends."*

The above verse is inscribed in the Claddagh ring, which was given to me by wife Darlene, and I use as my wedding ring. She knows it has special meaning to me (as I will explain below) and that we both acknowledge Christ's sacrifice and its meaning to our religious beliefs. There are also so many examples of those who have sacrificed and given up their lives, careers, things of meaning to others.

**Inspire:** Initially, I thought to write more on my uncle and namesake, Francis B. Burns, Corporal (CPL), United States Marine Corps (USMC), date of death 08 June 1951. Imagine visiting a cemetery as a youth and seeing a white marble veterans' stone with your name on it. Then, you look at the date of birth, the dash, and then the date of death. You kind of think a bit, and then realize that the date of death is your birthday—June 8th. As you look and reflect at the dash, you see CPL, USMC, and on the next line BSM (V) PH (2), which means Bronze Star Medal with Valor, and two Purple Hearts, the second of which resulted in his death. How can someone willingly give their life for others? How can I live up to that?

I then through of my mother who ingrained unto me, and my siblings, a deep sense of worship, primarily through personal example.

**Ignite:** Influence.

*Leominster, Massachusetts, 1947. My mother, A. Elizabeth (Frazier) Burns.*

## Back Azimuths

Below is my final farewell to mom given in 2017. I remember my mom as always being there for us. I spoke of the gifts that she gave to each of my siblings, in-laws, family, and friends. One of the last things she did before she passed, was that she crocheted afghans for every grandchild, made up of each grandchild's favorite colors. Her influence and love are now wrapped around her grandchildren even if she is not physically here with them.

*\*\*\**

*"Amen, amen, I say to you, unless a grain of wheat falls to the ground and dies, it remains just a grain of wheat; but if it dies, it produces much fruit."*
*(John 12: 24-25)*

*I am Francis, the eighth of nine children born to Liz Burns. It is wonderful to see so many relatives and friends here to join in the celebration of this funeral mass for our mother, and to rejoice that our mother's life, as the preface to today's mass states, is not taken away, but changed. We have a confident hope, as our faith teaches us, that a life led in sacrificial, devotional love, as hers was, will be rewarded with eternal bliss.*

*We all try to live a life of sacrificial, devotional love, and my mother's example has been a great aid in this; she has been an example of saintliness for all of us. If you visited her last week, in the final days of her life, you might have heard her tell you through her labored breathing that her death was near. It was not hard for her to tell this to her friends and family, because she had in fact lived every day with the end of her life in mind. The awareness that she would someday die is what led her to devote every moment of her life to God, with loving attention to the needs of her family, friends, and those less fortunate than she. You may have come to know her or to know her better through some of her devotional work, perhaps with the food pantry, or the prayer line, or the visiting nurses' association, or the parish women's guild, or the Giving Tree, or the Thanksgiving Food Drive, or the Pro-Life movement, in which you joined with her in the calling of Christian service, and thereby became her friend. Your friendship may go back many years, for some of you even back before the Second World War, or it may have been quite recent. Perhaps you were one of the neighborhood kids sent over with a cut or a sprain for her to attend to. Long or short, your friendship gave our mother joy.*

*We know through what we have heard from you this past week, and as we had heard from many people for a long time, that her love and courage sustained many people in their hours of need. We know that both by speech and deed she taught many to follow the path of righteousness. Growing up, though she worked nights as a nurse at the hospital and tended to our needs by day, the Lord seemed always to sustain her. I saw her sick only once. She was driving us somewhere. She pulled over the side of the road, opened her door, vomited, cleaned her face, and then kept driving to wherever it was that we were going. With so many people in need, it seemed, she had no time to be sick. She once gashed a finger open while cooking, and my sister Melanie asked her why she wasn't crying. "I cried out all my tears when I was a young girl," she replied. And there were too many tears of others to be wiped away. When she separated her right shoulder, the only noticeable change was that she made the Sign of Cross with her left hand. May our Church and our nation be given more souls like that of Lizzy Burns.*

*She gave many gifts, and she bequeathed gifts to each of her children. To Tom, whom we lost last year, she bequeathed the gift of being a caretaker, and he continued to the end to care for her yard. To Michael, she bequeathed the gift of generosity and of sharing stories, which he used when he called her from California every Sunday. To Rick, she bequeathed the gift of devoted work, which he used so well in the repair and upkeep of Mom's home. To Cathy, she gave the gift of attentive care, which she used so wonderfully to take care of our mother. To John, whom we also miss, she gave the gift of having a good sense of humor, and the good sense of knowing when to use it. To Tim, she gave the gifts of gardening, reading, and singing, so that he bothers everyone with his voice at masses. To Melanie, she bequeathed the gift of care-giving and holistic health, which she uses to make the lives of others better. To me, her June Rose, as she liked to call me, she gave the gift of lifelong learning and love of our fatherland, which I have worked to defend. To Patrick, she gave the gift of time, so that he dutifully carved time from his schedule to spend time with her.*

*To our spouses, and in-laws, she gave the gift of loving hospitality for holidays and feasts. To her grandchildren and great grandchildren, she gave the gift of affection, which they displayed to her on visits, making her face glow with joy. To our aunts and cousins, she gave the gift of familial love, and to her friends, the invaluable gift of friendship. Because she was an orphan, these friends also became our family, as we seemed to call everyone aunt or uncle. Pretty much everyone in the neighborhood on Litchfield Street & Calza Street, folks here at Holy Family, The Brasilis, The Bruces, The Basques, Lucky, and many more.*

*I began by quoting from the gospel of John: "A grain of what remains no more than a single grain unless it is dropped into the ground and dies. If it does die, it produces many grains."*

*Today, from the well of our sorrow filled with the tears of our loss, we will add nourishment to those many grains of wheat that our mother has sown, with her quiet virtues and her humility, as we learn to tend to our gardens, emboldened by the faith and trust in God that she exemplified and from which the joy and happiness and hope to which she aspired, will flower again.*

*Thank all you for being a part of our mother's wonderful life, and for being here with us today. Please join us for the burial at St. Leo's Cemetery, immediately following completion of the Mass. My brothers and sisters join me in inviting all of you to share in some fellowship and a meal at Christina's restaurant on Route 12 right after the burial.*

## Personal Reflection

- It is said that the fear of public speaking, is greater than death itself. Hence, Jerry Seinfeld has been quoted as saying that this in turn means that the one speaking would rather be in the casket than delivering a eulogy.
- I consider myself fortunate in that I have had the opportunity to write and deliver eulogies for family members. Sometimes I have volunteered, other times I have asked, sometimes I have been selected. As I left my hometown after college, I may be able to offer a different perspective, or see things through a different lens as it were.

## Contemplate

What has been inculcated or ingrained into you from your youth?

_____
_____
_____
_____
_____

What are some examples of your parents or grandparents that you still emulate?

_____
_____
_____
_____
_____

What is your go-to Bible verse and why? What is your go-to quote and why?

_____
_____
_____
_____
_____

# Workmanship

Performance of a laborer; performance of a particular task to piece of work.

**Insight:** Galatians 6:9.

*"Let us not grow tired of doing good, for in due time we shall reap our harvest, if we do not give up."*

I often write the first part of this verse is verse as a congratulatory remark to others when they have graduated, been promoted, received recognition for a job well done. It is a solid reminder that we should not rest upon our laurels, the past is last, and the only easy day was yesterday. We would do well to heed the words that were whispered in a Roman leader's ear when they returned from battle, *Momento Mori*, "Remember you must die."[63]

We have to be reminded to continue to put in the time, and the effort.

**Inspire:** The term sweat equity is used to describe putting in the effort to complete the job or project, whatever it may be. There is

---
63. The Obstacle Is the Way: The Timeless Art of Turning Trials into Triumph. Ryan Holiday. Portfolio. 2014.

often something physical that is involved in this term, and we release endorphins in work, in labor. To me, the taste of salt, be it in the form of sweat, blood, or tears is a reminder of the phrase from the Sermon on the Mount, "you are the salt of the earth." This means that those who labor—fisherman, shepherds, carpenters, and like my father tool and die makers—were virtuous people. In the days prior to refrigeration, salt was used to preserve food, and was indeed precious. In a sense, those whose example I have been able to witness possessed that preciousness.

**Ignite:** Silent example.

*Leominster, MA, circa 1946. My father (standing) and his siblings. Kneeling from left to right: Robert F. Burns, Theresa (Burns) Sangster, Rita (Burns) Oleson, and Francis B. Burns.*

In addition to my mothers' example of worship, my father set an example in workmanship. The letters that he wrote to my mother during WWII have offered a unique opportunity for me to appreciate a side of him that I, and others, did not know. I have included my eulogy I gave at his funeral Mass in December 2003, at Holy Family of Nazareth parish, in Leominster, MA.

\* \* \*

*Christian, Husband, Father, Grandfather, Brother, Uncle, Soldier, Mold-maker, Lector, Sports fan, oh excuse me — avid Red Sox Fan, Stubborn, Co-worker, Friend, Prankster, Neighbor, Cribbage Player, Patriarch.*

*What was / will he remain to you when you think of him? Duty, Loving, Loyal, Hard-working, Smoker, Selfless Service, Passionate, Disciplinarian?*

*Like most of you, I was unable to see him in the past couple of days. One of his last cogent thoughts on Friday night was to his daughter-in-law, Laura, to ensure that she was able to get Mammy a card and present for Christmas. Shortly thereafter, the main artery in his heart gave out, he started vomiting, was taken to Leominster Hospital, and then was air-evacuated to St Vincent's in Worcester. There a stint was emplaced in the upper left chamber of his heart. The physicians knew he had a damaged heart, and he probably had previously had a heart attack (may have been this past October after Bret Boone hit the extra inning homerun, or in 1986 with Bill Buckner, or in 1978 with Bucky Dent). Despite this, and respirators, pints of blood and fluid, his heart, lungs, and kidneys failed as he finally succumbed at around 1130 hours on Saturday, 13 December.*

*And so passed another hero of our Greatest Generation. Another one to not know what it's like to have the Red Sox win a World Series.*

*Ask that you not remember him in this way, or how he has*

*been the past few years' health wise, which has certainly affected his physical and mental functions.*

*What will be his legacy? How will he be remembered? What mark will he leave upon you?*

*I will offer you a perspective of the 8th of nine children. Since I'm in the service, I will shoot a back azimuth to recall some things that he did. Believe that he has been successful in that he has lived well, laughed often, and loved much, has filled his niche, and accomplished his task, and has left the world better than he found it.*

*Unlike my brother Tim, I possess neither that eloquence of diction, brilliance of metaphor, that poetry of imagination, to give a fitting eulogy for my father. Nonetheless…*

*You have read the obituary. Born Thomas Condon Burns, Jr., in Northampton, MA in 1925, eldest of five children. Lived through the Depression. His brothers and sisters were given up to the state early in his life, as his parents were divorced. Did not complete high school. Worked at the Hotel Northampton. Stayed in contact with his siblings by taking the train from Springfield. Believe that he somehow/ someway met his future wife during this time.*

*Off to war, over there, as he too Was a Soldier Once, and Young. Trained in England, sent a rose and many letters to Elizabeth Frazier while there. Landed on D-day plus 6. There he laid fuel lines for the Allied Advance… as he told me, "After every couple of miles, we had to go back and check for sabotage." "Marched all the way across France," as he was fond of saying. Was there in the Battle of the Bulge.*

*Came back to the states. Used the GI Bill to go to school for mold making and GI loan to build the house at 296 Litchfield after living in the projects for a few years. Worked at Foster*

*Grant, left there for a nickel per hour wage dispute. Continued his work at Crisci's, then at Leominster Tool & Die. Did work for Basque plastics, Jam Plastics, and many other tool and die companies.*

*Along with Ma, taught us to pray. Ma used to go to the 6:30 p.m. Mass with some of us on Saturdays, he took the rest of us to the 7:30 a.m. Mass on Sundays, singing without music accompaniment "Faith of our Fathers" and serving as either a Lector or Collector. He taught me to drive after church in the parking lot after Mass. Very active in the church, especially the Bishop's Fund. Remember many a phone calls made from 296. "Hello? Oh, this is Tommy Burns of Holy Family of Nazareth Parish. Was wondering if you can give us a hand with the annual Bishop's Fund? You can't? Oh, go to hell." Asked permission to take home a missallette from the church so that he wouldn't mispronounce Melchizedek; yet, he still mis-pronounced it. Had Father Hardy over for fried dough on Sunday night.*

*Instilled in us something to get our minds off the daily grind — a love for sports. Managed to coach Catholic Youth Council (CYC) basketball, Little League on 12th Street. His nickname Dutch came from the custodian at the Armory where he coached CYC basketball.*

*Attended every game that he was able — didn't miss a football game of mine or my brothers, or Melanie's basketball game, or Cathy's cheerleading during high school. Still picture him at Doyle Field or the Babe Ruth field in the bleachers, at baseball games in his green dickies, white t-shirt, slippers, smoking a Lucky Strike, watching the game.*

*Taught us to work. Through his daily discipline of getting up at 6 a.m., shaving with a cigarette in his mouth, eating his soft-boiled egg on toast, working his 55-hour+ weeks away from home, another 20-25 at his "work-shop" in the cellar, listening to country music on the A.M radio, or the "Echoes of Erin" program on Sunday mornings, while polishing dies and molds. Or being on the receiving end of his discipline by getting a good 'crack' for being so 'snotty'. Able to work those hours as Ma was working the night shift at the hospital. Cathy, Mrs. Basque, Brasili's all kind of looked out for each other.*

*He tried to set us up for success, not failure. He did not want all of that which had happened to him while he was growing up to happen to his family. He provided for us a Catholic education for 12 years through the Sisters of the Presentation of the Blessed Virgin Mary. Learned the Baltimore Catechism and memorized many prayers as well as Latin verbs and nouns. These prayers brought with them a heightened sense of community and sense of belonging.*

*He looked out for us. My sister Cathy and her husband Mark would say that he looked after some with a little more concern, especially in his long fur coat at CYC hayrides and sending us in to check on them while they were watching TV.*

*Active in the neighborhood. Put in a basketball court for us to play. Put in an above ground pool behind the house. The field in the backyard had many a neighborhood kid or little league team who played on it. Field also put into good use during the annual 4th of July party and inevitable kick-ball game.*

*Taught us about family and extended family. We called most all of Dad and Ma's friends Aunt and Uncle, though there were not many blood relations.*

*How to set an example. Mentorship, followership, friendship…*

*The 'atta-boy' 'you done good' or 'no-kiddin' were always well received by us.*

*Don't forget your ancestry. Trips to Northampton. JFK fifty-cent pieces, silver dollars, coal from the railroad track behind their house, penny candy from the market across the street. Going out to eat for us meant eating @ McDonald's or Hardee's (because I didn't like pickles).*

*Family vacations. Trips to Hampton Beach, Lexington-Concord, U.S.S. Massachusetts, Sturbridge Village. Getting lost on the way home from the beach, because "I don't want to go to Arlington." Pat pushing him down the hill when he was "making it rain."*

*Although not without faults with a Burns' sense of direction, Irish — Scot stubbornness, quick-temperedness, believe that his heart was in the right place, as he was able to encourage us in his own special way.*

*I carry something around with me in my work notebook. This is from 1994, when I was a Tactical officer at the United States Military Academy Preparatory School (USMAPS), located at Fort Monmouth, New Jersey. While there, we often had guest speakers come to the school to offer some insight into leadership. One of those who came was the first Medal of Honor Recipient in Vietnam, Colonel Roger H.C. Donlon (US Army, Retired).*

*On the surface, The Wedge Story is about Discouragement. What about Encouragement? Who possesses that?*

*I believe that we possess both. It is the constant fight inside each of use — the ying and the yang, the positive and negative, the two wolves, whatever analogy you want to use.*

*I have given a wedge to and shared the following story with others.*

Francis B. Burns

## The Wedge Story

*Once upon a time, the devil decided to have a sale. He offered his tools for sale to those who would pay the price.*

*On the night of the sale, they were all attractively displayed, a bad-looking lot. They were Malice, Hatred, Envy, Jealousy, Deceit and all the other implements of evil.*

*Apart from the rest lay a harmless wedge-shaped tool, much worn; yet priced higher than any of the others. Someone asked the Devil what it was.*

*"That is Discouragement," was the reply.*

*"Why do you have it priced so high?"*

*"Because," replied the Devil, "it is more to me than any of the others. I can pry open and get inside a man's conscience with that when I could not get near him with any of the others; and when once inside, I can use him in whatever way suits me best. It is so much worn because I use it with nearly everybody, as very few people yet know that it belongs to me."*

*It hardly needs to be added that the Devil had such a high price on Discouragement that it was never sold. He still owns it and is using it. Beware of it.*[64]

*Well, where's the other half of the wedge? If the Devil possessed Discouragement, where is the Encouragement?*

*In his own way, Dad possessed the opposite of discouragement... encouragement. Though a gentleman of few words, through his own personal example of excellence, let's be encouraged by what he did in this life, and that he has found happiness in the next.*

*Thank you.*

---

64. Personal Notes, 1995, United States Military Academy Preparatory School, (USMAPS), Fort Monmouth, New Jersey.

## Personal Reflection

- I was flooded with so many memories when I was writing this eulogy. I remember flying from Georgia to Massachusetts, and tears streaming down my face as I typed.
- The additional reminders of my father include the magni-focuser glasses, the smell of cigarette smoke, white t-shirts and Dickies pants, looking up into the stands of an athletic event in which I was playing and seeing him in the stands or on the sidelines.
- In a way, I believe that my father's use of the words "you done good" may have been his complimentary way of complementing GAL 6:9, "Do not tire of doing good."

Francis B. Burns

## Contemplate

Are your hands calloused? Scarred? Wrinkled? What work has made them so?

_____
_____
_____
_____
_____
_____

How has that work helped to shape you into who you are today?

_____
_____
_____
_____
_____
_____

How have the fruits of your labor helped to shape others?

_____
_____
_____
_____
_____
_____

# Membership

From the Latin meaning limb, part of the body; condition or status of a member of a society or (organized) body.

**Insight:** Luke 9:23.

*"If one wishes to come after me, he must deny himself and take up his cross daily and follow me."*

As many of the ... ships are interconnected, certainly membership is linked to partnership, followership, fellowship, relationship. It is important to belong to organizations that support your beliefs and values. With whatever organization to which we belong, we need to continue to discern that the mission and vision are in congruence with ours.

**Inspire:** In Lord Alfred Tennyson's poem, *Ulysses* (see page 62, Ambassadorship), the author remarks that, "I am part of all that I have met." In the poem, he bridges his heroic past with the uncertain future. He encourages others to join him and become shipmates with him once again. He wants them to not forget from where it is that they came and once again join him and be part of something bigger than themselves. To me, that defines membership.

**Ignite:** Don't forget your roots.

*Leominster, Massachusetts. Korean War Memorial.*
*My namesake's name is inscribed on the granite.*

Where you from? If you are speaking to me, my accent may not always give it away, I am often asked that question. In the summer of 2021, while Darlene and I were on vacation in Massachusetts, I was told by the server that I had a Kentucky accent. I laughed and replied with, "I'm from Le-mun-stah, you know, just north of Wus-tah!"

In 2010, I was asked to return to my hometown of Leominster, MA and give a speech for the Dedication Ceremony of the WW II and Korean War Memorial. Below is the speech that was delivered in June of that year.

## WWII and Korean Memorial Speech

*Good afternoon, and welcome again. Distinguished guests, thank you for allowing me to say a few words here today. Upfront I'll say some thank yous, share with you my linkage to this dedication, and offer some words to remember.*

*Thank all who contributed to make this day possible and all the donations from so many that made this memorial possible. Also, it is very fitting to have the Vietnam War Monument added to the other stones here at Carter Park.*

*It's a bit overwhelming to be here today. Looking across the street to St Leo's where I went to school from first to eight grades; seeing familiar faces; reading the names and trying to understand them. I have a direct link to one of the names on the monument. He is my namesake. United States Marine Corporal Francis Bernard Burns, killed in Korea, 8 June 1951, awarded a Bronze Star with Valor for living up to the words inscribed in my wedding ring, "Greater love has no one but this, that he lay down his life for his friends." I was born here, in Leominster, just a couple miles north of here, thirteen years to the day after he died.*

*The names on the monuments were known as Soldier, Marine, Sailor, Airmen, and Coastie. To us they were fathers, brothers, grandfathers, brother-in-laws, uncles, friends, neighbors. I will attempt to give them a fitting tribute to their lives that once were.*

*The names on the monuments are a cross section of our 111 citizens who bore the brunt of combat in WW II and in Korea. Leominster citizens gave their lives in defense of this country — a sacrifice Abraham Lincoln called a soldier's "last full measure of devotion."*

*As we look at the names on the monuments, we are reminded of a book of the Apocrypha, when Ecclesiastics wrote, "Honor and praise your famous men (and women)... those who have led and ruled wisely. They are deserving and have left names that their praises may be reported."*

*Yet at the same time, with less than ten percent of the US population having served in the Armed Services (and about one half on one percent currently serving), there remains a pang of guilt when contemplating those who do serve. Still, many of us try to imitate our grandparents and parents and family and friends whose values and work ethic we increasingly eulogize.*

*What did they miss?*
- *Marriages to their Sweetie Pies*
- *Birthday parties*
- *First steps*
- *Learning to ride a bike*
- *Going fishing*
- *Little League Football*
- *Pop Warner Football*
- *Girls and Boy Scouts activities*
- *Their kids' first dates, proms*
- *Going to college and opening a business*
- *Coming Home*

*I'll share some words from letters written back to Leominster, that my mom gave to me, oops, that I took from the cellar a few years ago after my dad passed away. One is from my father who was able to return from WW II and experience those things previously mentioned, and one is from his brother, my uncle, my namesake.*

*Dad, then a Private First Class in the 469th Maintenance Company, sent this letter from the War & Navy Departments, V-Mail service, postmarked 15 June 1944, and written to Miss Elizabeth Frazier, whom I call mom: My Dearest Darling Betty: There is a fellow in our company making bets that we will be home by the 4th of July. I hope he wins them all... I am going to write to my brothers and sisters... I still love you darling with all my heart. I prayed for you in church and am always thinking of you. I can't wait till the day when I see you again... With all my love, Tommy. P.S. I love you from the deepest part of my heart.*

*Uncle Francis, then a Private First Class with the 1st Marine Division, sent his letter via US Army Postal Service, postmarked 2 January 1951, written to my parents: Dear Tom & Liz: I received your package and am very grateful... It's really cold here at night... I had guard duty on Christmas from 12-6... We had really swell chow. The Army feeds like us like kings, of course we are kings here, anyway... Hope everyone is alright there, as I'm fine... Love to all, Francis.*

*A few months later, that letter from my Uncle Francis was followed by a letter from the President, and is one which many may have read, heard, or perhaps received. "In grateful memory of Francis Bernard Burns, who died in the service of his country on 8 June 1951 in Korea. He stands in the unbroken line of patriots who have dared to die that freedom might live, and grown, and increase its blessing. Freedom lives, and through it, he lives — in a way that humbles the undertaking of most men. Signed Harry Truman, President of the United States of America."*

*It's similar in tone to that which was sent from President*

*Abraham Lincoln to Mrs. Lydia Bixby on November 21, 1864.*

*Dear Madam, —I have been shown in the files of the War Department a statement of the Adjutant General of Massachusetts, that you are the mother of five sons who have died gloriously on the field of battle.*

*I feel how weak and fruitless must be any words of mine which should attempt to beguile you from the grief of a loss so overwhelming. But I cannot refrain from tendering to you the consolation that may be found in the thanks of the Republic they died to save.*

*I pray that our Heavenly Father may assuage the anguish of your bereavement and leave you only the cherished memory of the loved and lost, and the solemn pride that must be yours, to have laid so costly a sacrifice upon the altar of Freedom.*

*Yours, very sincerely and respectfully, Abraham Lincoln*

*Our freedom has been acquired by men who knew their duty and had the courage to do it. A veteran—whether active duty, retired, National Guard, or Reserve—is someone who, at one point in his or her life, wrote a blank check made payable to The United States of America, for an amount of up to and including my life. That is honor, and there are way too many people in this country who no longer understand it.*

*As the troops used to say, "If the country is good enough to live in, it's good enough to fight for." With privilege goes responsibility.*

*To the veterans being in attendance today, thank you for your service. You are in turn offering a living tribute to our comrades. Death ends a life, but never a relationship. We all have but one death to spend, and insofar as it can have any* meaning, it finds it in the service of comrades in arms. Perhaps part of us actually dies when we deploy.

You veterans can probably close your eyes and still hear the following phrases, itching at your ears until you understand them:

*I would have liked to live…*

*Take care of those guys…*

*Earn this…*

*If I failed as a leader, and I pray I didn't, it was not because I did not try…*

*I loved you, with all my heart…*

With you I am also reminded of a poem by Edward Markham that reads,

"There is a destiny that makes us brothers,
None goes his way alone,
All that we give to the lives of others,
Comes back into our very own."[65]

From World War (WW) II we remember Pearl Harbor, D-Day, battles in Africa and Europe, Island hopping campaign in the Pacific, or "Over there." The nickname for the Korean War has been the Forgotten War, today it, and those who gave the ultimate sacrifice in WW II, Korea, and those names on the Vietnam Memorial are no longer forgotten. I believe that our duty here today is to remember. We have an obligation to those veterans whose names are etched on these monuments, and veterans of all wars, to remember.

Pay attention to the ways in which your relationship con-

---

65. Creed poem. Edward Markham. Retrieved February 1, 2022 from https://www.poemhunter.com/poem/a-creed-3/.

*tinues, for to live in hearts we leave behind is not to die. What you do for yourself dies with you. What you do for others' lives forever.*

*Do not let any of their names become empty memories. Recall to your mind their good points, the many things we admire in them. Imitate them. In that way, their lives will be perpetuated among us. Our monument to them will not be of bronze or marble, but the living monument of all the good we saw in them.* [66]

*In remembering our fallen, we are reminded of our Greek origin, in words spoken over 2,400 years ago, in which Pericles is invited to speak after a famous battle to address the state of the nation and also the character of Soldiers. I quote:*

*"The Soldiers whose name are on the monument gave their lives for the common good, and thereby won for themselves praise that never grows old, and the most distinguished of all graves, not those in which they lie, but where their glory remains in eternal memory, always there at the right time to inspire speech and action."* [67]

*"Never in the field of human conflict, has so much, been owed by so many, to so few!"*

**Winston Churchill—September 1940**

*In closing, we often remember the dash when we visit cemeteries. It's the one in between the date of birth and date of death. We are reminded how we live that dash, and that's how we'll be remembered. Here, next to the names our monuments, is*

---

66. Grunt Padre 141.

67. Thucydides, Pericles' Funeral Oration. Retrieved February 1, 2022 from http://hrlibrary.umn.edu/education/thucydides.html.

*more of an invisible semi-colon, as their lives are weaved into our own.*

*May God continue to bless those service members who are deloyed and their families, as well as these veterans, their families, the Commonwealth of Massachusetts, and the United States of America! Thank you.*

Francis B. Burns

## Personal Reflection

- Don't forget your roots. There is always something from which to be gained when you go back.
- Be a good Teammate.
- Pay it forward.

## Contemplate

In what ways have you have given back to the community where you were raised?

_____
_____
_____
_____
_____

Describe the emotions that were evoked by recollecting what this means to you?

_____
_____
_____
_____
_____

Describe a way in which you a part of something bigger than yourself?

_____
_____
_____
_____
_____

# Sportsmanship

(10) Pleasant pastime; entertainment or amusement; recreation or diversion.
(8) Participation is games or exercises, especially those of the athletic character.

**Insight:** Joshua 1:9.

> *"I command you: Be strong and steadfast! Do not fear or be dismayed, for the Lord, your God, is with you wherever you go."*

There is something about an imperative sentence that demands instruction through the use of few words. You, as in the form of the 2nd Person, are the subject. By commanding that you become strong and courageous, the verse implies that you know what the words mean, and that after learning them, you use them in a positive manner. Being strong and courageous is part of sports, and in turn, sportsmanship.

There are so many exceptional coaches from which to draw lessons. Having spent time in the proverbial arena allows us to experience the meaning of the coaches' words.

**Inspire:** My initial thoughts on sportsmanship were to the sport of rugby, of which I played for several years in Europe and in the

States and wrote about in marksmanship. Related to rugby is American football. Prior to our Saturday afternoon high school football games at St. Bernard's Central Catholic High School in Fitchburg, Massachusetts, (we rarely had Friday Night Lights in Massachusetts in the early 1980s), the team would gather and have Mass celebrated for us. Afterwards, the seniors would go to a home (sometimes my parents') or to a restaurant for breakfast. It was during Senior Talks, when the seniors would get the opportunity to share some thoughts prior to the final contest. During my talk, I used this quote from US Army General Douglas C. MacArthur, "Upon the fields of friendly strife are sown the seeds, which, upon other fields, on other days, will bear the fruits of victory" in high school. I shared them on Thanksgiving Eve, 1981, when after the celebration of Mass for our football game, the seniors gave our Senior Talks. I believe that I was hinting at the practices, and maybe a bit towards using sports as an analogy for life. In the words of the Olympic Creed, "Life is about the struggle, not the triumph."

**Ignite:** Intangibles.

*Concord, Massachusetts, 1957. Walter A. Carew, Jr.*

## Back Azimuths

I delivered the below message at a Youth Sports Banquet, at Fort Polk, Louisiana in 2009. It afforded me the opportunity to address the young athletes, the coaches, and the parents. I did not address the number of tackles, touchdowns, points scored, won / loss record. I tried to address the intangibles that sports teach.

\* \* \*

*I appreciate having the opportunity to say a few words tonight. I almost broke out my 1977 Leominster Pop Warner jacket and put it on for the occasion. I have great memories of my time spent in youth football.*

*Schoolwork, good character, good behavior come first.*

*Sports are a complementary and beneficial extracurricular activity.*

*John and the Child and Youth Sports Service Staff. Thank you for stepping up this fall, and not allowing the program to fail. Thank you for being there for the kids.*

*Parents / guardians. Thank you for allowing your children the opportunity to play football this fall. I've heard some of the kids say, "I like to have my mom and dad watch me play, as long as they behave." Thanks for understanding that, "Upon the fields of friendly strife are sown the seeds that, upon other fields, on other days, will bear the fruits of victory."*

*Coaches. Thank you. At times, you wondered whether you'd rather be coaching, or testing body armor for bullet penetration. The coach is, first of all, a teacher. A teacher affects eternity; he can never tell where his influence stops.*

*Chalk, talk, walk, run; crawl, walk run; name, explain, demonstrate, conduct practical use in ... Athletes do not win on emotion, they win on proper mechanics.*

*Players: You have learned about Character:*

*First, those 4/10 stickers you wore on the back of your helmets, representing the 3,350 Soldiers who are fighting in Afghanistan, many of which are your fathers or mothers. They are wearing gear like you did, a bit heavier, and are playing an "Away" game for about 12 months, so that the fight will not become a "Home" game.*

- *Learned about not being afraid to fail, but not making the same mistake twice*
- *Learned that competition means to strive together, not against each other.*
- *Learned about Teamwork, playing hard, playing aggressive.*
- *Learned that you can give 100%, but if one guy is out of position then someone's running through the line of scrimmage and he's going to gain a bunch of yards.*

*1. Sights, Smells, and Sounds:*
- *The sound of cleats on a hard surface, whether on a newly waxed kitchen floor you weren't supposed to be walking on or on pavement. When you wore cleats, you felt tall, strong.*
- *What about the sound of helmets and shoulder pads smacking together—as you wait breathlessly, nervously for the contest to finally begin.*
- *The solid thumps of a solo tackle, or a team effort of thumps in the pile?*
- *The smell of chewed up dirt, mud—on your hands, clothes, cleats.*
- *The smell of a football itself.*

- *Every sting, hit, and impact.*

*2. Striving: whether it be to win, for excellence, to improve yourself. To practice, practice, practice over and over again. Like endless sprints at the end of a long exhausting practice when you can barely lift your neck above your shoulder pads, arms and the sweat is dripping down your face, salt stinging your eyeballs. It's that feeling you have when you've given your all, when there's nothing left, your whole-body aches and tingles from the reaching, the running, trying, and striving.*

*3. Sportsmanship. I was happy and probably very lucky to play on teams where sportsmanship mattered, from the top on down. That's because the coaches I had cared more about being decent and playing well instead of winning at any cost, especially the sacrifice of your opponent's (and ultimately your own) dignity. I trust that things are the same now 33 years later, that you hold out your hand, not only to the other side at the end of the game in the obligatory handshake, but that, during the game, you extend your hand to your opponent when he has fallen down because it's the right thing to do. This is so much bigger than how you conduct yourself on the field. It's a question of who you want to be, who you decide to be.*

*4. Loss / Suffering. Organized athletics became an easy way for me to learn what loss / suffering is about. Success does not breed success; it breeds failure. It is failure, which breeds success. No matter what we do in life, we are all going to have wins and losses! But the wins do not require us to reach down inside ourselves and find qualities that we never knew we had. But the losses do! It is in defeat; in the anguish of coming up short that we are faced with opportunities to grow as athletes and as human beings.*

*I still remember one of my Pop Warner football games when we travelled to Waltham, MA to play a game. When we arrived and were departing, we were told by the coaches to put our helmets on when we are on the bus, as the previous Leominster team had had its bus stoned with rocks. You see, in 1977, we had an integrated team, and the city and the team that we were playing were still struggling with racial issues.*

*5. Friendship. There probably isn't enough I could say about the friendships I have gained playing sports. The solidarity among my teammates as we forged both our individual identities and a class consciousness of ourselves as young men is invaluable.*

*The total of those things that I just mentioned is summed up in one word — Character. Your involvement in team sports happened during some of the formative years of your lives — between ages 7 and 14.*

*I'll close with a short prayer that we used to say when I was in high school, taught to us by Coach Walter Carew, my high school football coach. He was a US Army Infantry CPT in WW II, got out, started raising a family, was re-called for Korean War, and fought in Korea. He came back and coached Concord High football team to a 59-0 win streak — undefeated over six straight seasons. Retired from coaching and teaching, then came back and coached at a small private high School in Fitchburg, Massachusetts. That is where our lives crossed — from 1979-1982. He was also an English teacher who enjoyed poetry (lived about ten minutes from Walden Pond).*

*What we said before and after every game: "Lord, help us to grow in love and respect for one another, and for all with whom we come in contact; especially those that need us. Help us to appreciate how much we really need each other."*[68]

*That quote is next to my picture in my high school yearbook and is the same prayer I say with my children before they go to sleep.*

*Congratulations on your achievements.*

*Congratulations on the development of your character.*

*In sports, understand that the life lessons learned are more important than fundamentals.*

*Thank you.*

---

68. Burns Personal Notes.

## Personal Reflection

- Related to membership, always be part of something bigger than yourself. Always be a part of a team.
- It's about teamwork.
- It's about the trials of miles, miles of trials, found in John Parker's book, *Once a Runner*.
- It's about the process.
- Don't let them see you in pain.
- If you get knocked down, dust yourself off, recover.
- US Army Brigadier General Pat Work, who served as a Captain of the United States Military Academy (USMA) football team in 1995, has a way of expressing doing your part, "Do your 1/11th."[69]

---

69. Brigadier General Pat Work, Mantras, Apple Podcast. May 22, 2021. Retrieved May 23, 2021, from https://podcasts.apple.com/us/podcast/64-brigadier-general-pat-work-mantras-to-center-your/id1468715294?i=1000523029288.

Back Azimuths

## Contemplate

What are the best sports expressions that I have heard?

_____
_____
_____
_____
_____

What are my lessons learned from the fields of friendly strife to my life?

_____
_____
_____
_____
_____

In what way(s) do I appreciate and apply these lessons in my life?

_____
_____
_____
_____
_____

# Hardship

Rigor; severity; painful difficulty.

**Insight:** 2 Timothy 2:3.

*"Bear your share of hardship along with me like a good soldier of Christ Jesus."*

As with sportsmanship, we often learn more from loss, suffering, or pain. This allows us to acknowledge that the pain suffered on this earth, and that Christ has sacrificed for us. I have often prayed for the suffering of family and friends to be instead re-directed to me, so that I could ease their burden.

**Inspire:** We all have suffered and endured hardships. We all have experienced positive and negative events in our lives, such as death of a loved one, observing / witnessing / or being part of catastrophic events, separation, divorce, or something that stirs our emotions to another level. Perhaps some of us have a one-time event, which has formed us in a positive or negative way. In the USMC, new recruits are put through "The Crucible" to culminate their 12-weeks of initial entry training. There may be schools we have attended that have pushed to our spiritually, physically, emotionally, mentally. I believe it is not the event itself that is critical or hard, it is how we react to that event that matters. In essence, hardship builds resiliency.

**Ignite:** Embrace the suck.

*Fort Benning, Georgia, 2005 One Station Unit Training (OSUT) receiving their crossed rifles, after having completed their final foot march.*

During my time served at Fort Benning, Georgia, besides the mandatory classes on the Uniform Code of Military Justice (UCMJ) and Law of Land Warfare, Infantry One Station Unit Training (OSUT) Soldiers were shown short excerpts from recent films in order to establish an ethical/ moral foundation, as from my experience, not every Soldier had a firm background prior to coming into the Army. These film excerpts showed how a particular value related to something that the Soldier may have already seen / experienced. The senior officer in the unit (battalion commander) taught these classes, with the entire cadre present, and offered Socratic questions as a means of shaping each Soldier's moral compass. This initial values training built the Soldiers' concept of duty, or a willingness to commit to a larger cause, and implied a sense of belonging and togetherness. It was a first step in the inculcation and habituation, or doing the right thing, in the right manner, for the right reasons. This is also in line with a phrase from Will Durant, who summarized some of Aristotle's thoughts in this manner, "We are what we repeatedly do. Excellence, therefore, is not an act, but a habit."[70]

Additionally, some infantry training companies in 1st Battalion, 50th Infantry Regiment at Fort Benning, Georgia, used to have an 'Army Value of the Week' and taught additional case studies that reinforce an Army value. Soldiers were reminded that when they return home, they will be the ones who are changed — not their homes — as they will now look at things through different (read military) lenses. Since these classes are initially taught within the first week of arrival, it provokes the new Soldiers to ask who they are and compare it to who and / or what they will become. Or, put another way, they re-learn what they already know.

Army values also were reinforced by other means. One of our companies, Charlie Company, 1st Battalion, offered "legacy cards" to the newly arrived Soldiers. These were three by five index cards, carried in a Ziploc bag, which had the name, short biography, and the obituary of a Soldier from that unit who was killed in Vietnam. Each Soldier carried that card with him for the entire fourteen weeks, and then presented the card back at a ceremony at the battalion's Vietnam memorial following completion of the final field

---

70. Aristotle Quote. Retrieved December 29, 2008 from https://medium.com/the-mission/my-favourite-quote-of-all-time-is-a-misattribution-66356f22843d.

training exercise. It was quite a moving experience in the fourteen weeks of the new Infantryman's hardship and yet it paled in comparison to the sacrifice of those names on the legacy cards.

I offered the below speech to the Vietnam Veterans of 1st Battalion, 50th Infantry Regiment. These teammates were drafted together, shared many hardships, and now get together bi-annually for their reunion.

\* \* \*

*Thank you for attending today's Wreath Laying Ceremony.*

*I would like to recognize and thank Ms. Christine Spaulding for the singing of the National Anthem, and Ms. Jennifer Robinson and Ms. Keisy Dillard for providing the music for today's ceremony. There are two pieces of music that particularly stir the hearts and emotions of Americans — The Star-Spangled Banner and Taps. You represent the future of our country, and we thank you for being a special part of today's ceremony. Also, Chaplain Van Ness — thank you for your prayer which fostered a heightened sense of community and belonging to all of us gathered here today.*

*Today we are specifically recognizing the Veterans of the 1st Battalion, 50th Infantry, at this wreath laying ceremony. It is a significant day, in that, on this day in 1968, the Battalion participated in the Battle of An Bao. Some of those Soldiers names in front of us today are from that battle.*

*For most of the veterans and their families and loved ones, it may be the first time that you have seen the monument that was dedicated last year. It may also be the first time for the*

*Soldiers standing behind you today to have participated in such a Ceremony.*

*When you think of veterans, what first comes to your mind? Is it an older gentleman, in a not-so-good fitting uniform, wearing a hat that represents the unit to which he was assigned, or someone wearing an American Legion, VFW, or Vietnam Veteran hat at a parade, walking the street? Distributing poppies at a grocery store, or someone you know who is in a Soldiers home?*

*Or is it, as for me, visiting family gravesides, seeing the white marble slabs with American flags? After your prayers at the graveside, you probably ask yourself what is his legacy? How will he be remembered? What mark did he leave on his fellow comrades? What impact will he leave upon you?*

*The veteran that you have in mind... What was, or, will remain to you when you think of him or her? How will you be remembered? How do you want to be remembered? What legacy will you leave behind?*

*The veterans whose names are etched on the monument before you — men such as PFC Freidt, SPC Holloway, SGT Fullam — will remain forever young, an average age of about 27. About the about the same age as Fox Company cadre CPT Powell, Drill Sergeants Sloss, Owens, Hill, or Fox Company Soldiers — Privates Adcock, Bachand, Carr, or Steven.*

*In my search on the internet, in books, and jogging my memory, there were many examples of what to say at such a ceremony. This morning, I have chosen one word, character. It is the unwritten Army value, or the backbone of the Army Values, as the Non-Commissioned Officers are considered the backbone of the Army. I will offer one brief excerpt of a funeral oration or a tribute.*

*Character certainly has military ties. Having recently attended some military retirement ceremonies, it almost seems as if those are, in a way, a living tribute to one whom has dedicated a lifetime of service to our nation. By the veterans being in attendance today, you are in turn offering a living tribute to your comrades.*

*In the military, we have many traditions, one of which is called a Hail & Farewell. For some it is the first and last time that one will see the person, as Soldiers and families rotate through different Army units. Today some of us will be offering a hail and farewell to those who have given the ultimate sacrifice for us. (I then read Catullus' poem here, and I will not repeat it here. It is found on page 59.)*

*Thank you for remembering our veterans and comrades.*

*May God continue to bless them, the veterans and families of the 1st Battalion 50th Infantry, the US Army, and the United States of America.*

*Thank you.*
"PLAY THE GAME"
"FIX BAYONETS"

## Personal Reflection

- We all have two things in common: we all have experienced both elation and suffering in our lives.
- I really try to pay attention, and often take notes at retirement, memorial dedications, graduations, and recognition ceremonies in order to garner the message being delivered.
- I echo Marcus Aurelius' thoughts in that, "Every day more of life is used up and less and less of it is left."

## Contemplate

What is a crucible event(s) in your life that has shaped you?

_____
_____
_____
_____
_____

What were the lessons learned from these events?

_____
_____
_____
_____
_____

What are some ways to safely impart some of these lessons for future generations?

_____
_____
_____
_____
_____

# Citizenship

Inhabitant of a city or (often) of a town, especially one possessing civic rights and privileges.

**Insight:** Matthew 15:212.

*"Then repay to Caesar what belongs to Caesar, and to God what belongs to God."*

This verse is referred to as the 'The Tribute Episode.' I first learned of this Bible verse when I was a sophomore in high school. It was an extra credit question on Shakespeare's Julius Caesar exam. When the Pharisees asked Jesus about paying a census tax, he rendered this thought on whether it was lawful to give tribute to Caesar or not. The context behind what Jesus was saying is that things of God and Caesar are mutually exclusive. As he often did, Jesus followed up the question by asking about the image and inscription on the coin. In doing so, he distinguished the difference between paying tribute to God and Caesar.

When I read more about this verse, it occurred to me that unique to the United States currency is that we have images of distinguished US citizens on the front side of the coin, and we have the words "In God We Trust" as well as *e pluribus unum* (one from many) inscribed on the currency.

**Inspire:** In this talk, I mention Army Lieutenant Colonel Brian Birdwell. In December of 2021, at the invitation of our youngest son, and on behalf of the Baylor Army Reserve Officer Training Corps (ROTC), now Texas State Senator Birdwell addressed the Baylor Bear Army ROTC Battalion at its December Dining Out. It gave me a sense of pride that our son wrote the letter inviting Senator Birdwell to the event, researched his life, and read Senator and Mrs. Birdwell's book, *Refined By Fire*, in preparation of writing the introduction of Senator Birdwell at the event. Lastly, in that our son was only six months' old on 9/11, it gave me a bit of closure as well as a rekindling of some of the ash from that day into developing citizens.

**Ignite:** Connectivity with others.

# Back Azimuths

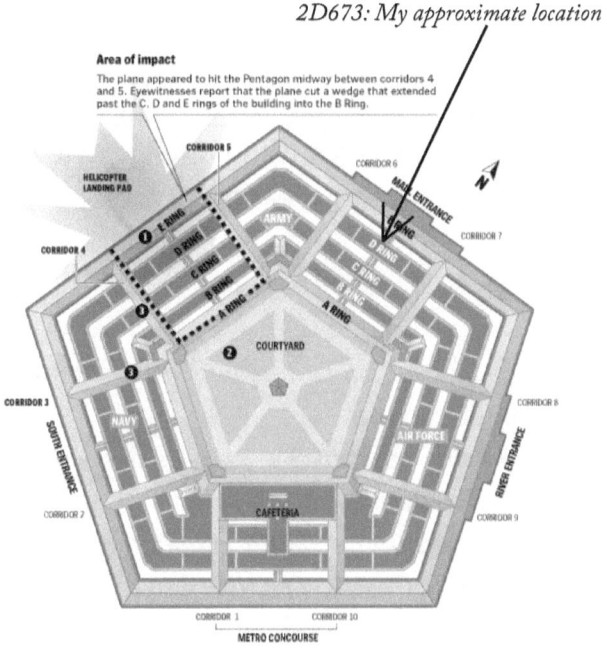

*Pentagon Map depicting area of impact on 9/11.*

This is the transcript from a 9/11 talk from September 2020 that was recorded without an audience (due to COVID-19) at Saint John Paul II (SJPII) Catholic High School, in Schertz, Texas. I think I was more nervous without an audience than one being there with whom to engage. I had previously written down and spoke a bit on my experiences of 9/11 and thought that this may be the best way to capture my thoughts and emotions of the day and then the years that followed. I often refer to this as a 'duty' speech or the 'ing' / Imperfect Tense speech, as it describes events as they were happening

I am grateful for SJPII's Principal, Mr. Andrew Iliff for not only recording and the editing, and insertion of many photos throughout the talk. He, along with other Catholic School educators have been very influential in our families' lives.

The hyperlink to the talk is found at: https://www.linkedin.com/in/francis-b-burns-86ab736/overlay/1608576309217/single-media-viewer/?type=LINK&profileId=ACoAAAE9dBIB-J4E5XmrBUEOjcH_3vXK_oGnykmY/

\*\*\*

*Good morning and thank you for allowing me to say a few words this morning.*

*9/11/2001. I believe that the students here were not born yet, correct? Nonetheless, what do you picture? Planes used as weapons; thousands of lives lost; buildings burning; huge structures collapsing; disbelief, shock, a terrible sadness, and a quiet, unyielding anger. Citizens from 90 countries lost their lives in NYC, at The Pentagon, and in a field in Shanksville, PA.*

*As we reflect on that day, we remember that a ruthless enemy maliciously attacked our country as they attempted to crush our will to stand up to protect the ideals of liberty and humanity. Yet, they underestimated America's resolve.*

*I was present at The Pentagon on 9/11. However thankful I am to have walked away without a scratch, at the same time I have experienced the grief and guilt, when others lost life, limbs, and more. That grief and guilt has in turn allowed me to experience God's grace.*

*Why am I speaking this morning? Elie Wiesel, an Auschwitz survivor, reminds us that, "Whoever survives a test, whatever it may be, must tell the story. That is his duty." So, I am here.*

*Here we go…*

## Back Azimuths

*Midway in the journey of our life*
*I came to myself in a dark wood,*
*For the straightway was lost.*

*From what book is that? — Dante's Inferno. With all epics that you read here, such as The Divine Comedy, The Odyssey, and The Iliad, The Aeneid, and Beowulf — they all start In Medias Res.*

*We will begin on Tuesday, September 11th, 2001. Looking back now, it was the exact midpoint, or midway of my 30-year Active Army career, having entered Active Duty 11 September 1986. In Medias Res…*

*I was somewhat spiritually, emotionally, and physically drained, as over the weekend I had attended the wake and funeral of a fellow rugby player up in Pennsylvania — not too far from where Todd Beamer would utter the now famous quote of "Let's Roll!"*

*That morning, after watching footage of both planes hitting the World Trade Towers, I remember calling a buddy of mine who worked in the Deputy Secretary of Defense (Paul Wolfowitz's) office and asking him what was happening. He told me "We're tracking more, I'll call you back." I never got the return call.*

*Later that morning, as we began our 0900 staff meeting, there are some quotes I will never forget:*

- *"Those towers will never come down." From a board-certified Engineer.*
- *At 0937, an 80-ton, Boeing 757, Flight # 77, slammed into the building at 530 miles-an-hour, with 3,000 pounds of jet fuel and 53 passengers & 6 crew members. The plane hit in*

*Corridor 4 and made it to Corridor 5. I worked in Corridor 6, just one corridor away.*

- *184 lives were lost immediately, many more were wounded. You may not know that the wall of the Pentagon that was hit had been recently rebuilt. In contrast to the poured concrete of the rest of the building, the section that was hit had blast-proof windows, reinforced steel in the concrete, and a sprinkler system. That part of the structure had just been occupied in August, and actually stood up for over 30 minutes, which in turn, prevented further damage and saved lives.*
- *"That's the aftershock of an explosion. We need to get the blank out of here." From a retired Explosive Ordnance Sergeant, who, from his experience, knew exactly what was happening.*
- *"Get off your computer, we need to go." It seemed that some folks remained oblivious to what was going on.*
- *As we exited our office, there was an Army Lieutenant Colonel directing us away from the blast site to another exit. I saw him some time later with bandages on both arms.*
- *Passing by another Lieutenant Colonel, this one from the Marine Corps, who was standing on top of the exit turnstiles and using some choice words with the security guards, who would not open the doors because they said, "They could only be opened in an emergency."*
- *Linking up at our rendezvous point, accounting for all in the office. Yes, fire and emergency drills do work. Our boss telling us to stay in touch via email, as we did for a week or so, and then doing what is commonplace since the COVID-19 outbreak—teleworking.*
- *Asking myself (to this day) if discretion was the better part of valor?*

- *Turning away from the flames, still not knowing what had happened or who was left in the building, or if I had missed my kairos moment?*
- *Walking across Memorial Bridge (over the Potomac River), in uniform, when a policeman on horseback told me that, "You'd better change out of your uniform, as we didn't know who else may be targeted."*
- *Stopping in at a building in DC to change. It turned out to be a Paralyzed Veterans Center. Seeing a former Lieutenant (student) of mine, who was paralyzed after a hard parachute landing fall at Fort Bragg a year earlier.*
- *Attempting to enter the Metro station to catch the train. Contrary to reports, it wasn't running at the time.*
- *Wondering about how to get home, as I had only been there for a couple of months, and I took the Metro every day.*
- *Wanting to rent a bicycle in Georgetown to ride home, but the rental owner wanted to physically hold my credit card as collateral, so I literally hit the trail that is parallel to Rock Creek Parkway.*
- *Listening (on my Sony Walkman) to words of the Twin Towers collapsing on my walk from the Pentagon to Silver Spring, MD.*
- *Praying and thinking about my family—how they were, where they were. The oldest, then seven-years old, was a student at St John's Catholic elementary school in Silver Spring, and the principal there was Sr. Mary Lannack, our rugby coach's aunt.*
- *Trying to get home, and for hours, attempting to call Darlene, and my family. Yes, there were cell phones then, but there was no text messaging, and all the cell towers were overloaded.*

- *Getting through to my mother, via a pay phone, whom I told that I loved, and asked her to call Darlene and tell her likewise and that all was well.*
- *Finishing the trek, my 12-plus mile plus foot march home, and hugging and kissing Darlene and the kids as they came to pick me up.*
- *Speaking with and emailing family and friends who had expressed their concern.*
- *Seeing the giant flag draped over the side of the Pentagon as I entered the building two days later (will speak more on flags in a bit).*
- *Smelling the charred ruins as I was sneaking into the office, under the yellow tape, to get some stuff off my desk, and then donating a pint of blood as I left the building.*
- *Attending the 10/11 Pentagon Memorial Ceremony with President Bush, and an Army General who started off by saying, "Soldier, Marine, Sailor, Airmen, Coast Guardsmen, Civilian, Contractor, Father, Mother, Brother, Sister, Husband, Wife, Aunt, Uncle, Niece, Nephew, Co-workers, Christian, Jewish, Muslim — PATRIOTS all — lost here last month. President Bush stating that on September 11th, 1941, was when Pentagon construction started.*
- *Visiting a co-worker, Brian Birdwell, at George Washington Burn unit, as he was burned on over 60% of his body. His head was incredibly large — the size of a melon. He was on his way to the latrine (restroom) when the plane hit — everyone else in that office was killed. As Brian was engulfed in diesel and flames, his polyester uniform was burned to his skin. When four men found him and tried to pick him up, his flesh was similar to hot glue, and it just peeled right off of him. The only thing that saved him, as he was crawling on*

*his burned hands and knees to the courtyard, was that he was old school—he wore the old black leather shoes, not the plastic corfram (ready shine) shoes. His feet were the only place on his body that was not burned, so that is where the IVs were eventually stuck. His job was the one for which I had interviewed a few months earlier and was supposed to be in when I arrived at the Pentagon. I ended up in another office instead. Brian is now a state Senator for Texas, with an office in Waco, near Baylor, where our oldest son (Conor) graduated, Cavan is now attending, and where one of my brothers, a former colleague of Dr. Gorman at 'then SW Texas State,' is now teaching.*

- *Escorting family and friends as they came to visit the Pentagon, including stopping and praying at the chapel.*
- *Sitting on one of the 184 benches outside of the Pentagon, each one representing one of the lives lost that day, offering prayers for those we lost, and remembering the quote that, "They gave all of their todays for our tomorrows."*
- *Receiving and sending the yearly emails on 9/11 from all in the office where I worked.*
- *Visiting Marines and Soldiers at Walter Reed Army Hospital, Bethesda Naval Hospital, and Brooke Army Medical Center. Two Soldiers with whom I had previously served stand out, as they are both double amputees: John Fernandez (whom I had coached in lacrosse at West Point Prep School) and then Tim Karcher (with whom I had rolled a bit in jiu-jitsu at Fort Benning and then served with him at Fort Hood & Iraq).*
- *Spending time in the office where I was that day, as I had subsequently been re-assigned to The Pentagon, to the same*

*organization. There are pictures and a memorial hanging on the wall of the office where our co-workers lost their lives.*
- *Attending memorial ceremonies, too many to remember, in the week, months, and now years that have followed, for those who gave the ultimate sacrifice.*
- *Viewing many flag-draped coffins, both here and while deployed, as each one gets harder to focus on the sacrifice rendered.*
- *Watching as a General Officer presents a flag to the deceased family at the graveside service for Soldiers who gave the ultimate sacrifice in combat in the Global War on Terror.*
- *Honoring and greeting the flag-draped coffins of fallen Soldiers at Randolph Air Force Base and San Antonio Airport.*
- *Flags have a special meaning to me, as I have the flag which my namesake, USMC Corporal Francis B. Burns, had draping on his coffin, after having given his life in the Korean War on June 8, 1951 so that others could be evacuated. I was born 13 years later, hence, a sense of calling was implanted in me to serve others.*
- *Deploying for over 31 months in the Global War on Terror*
- *Sharing with students, Veterans Organizations, Rotary Clubs, Auburn University Honors College the duties of citizenship and all that it entails.*
- *Reaching out with sports teams and giving an analogy about wearing 80-100 lbs. of gear and playing away games vs. home games, and how we don't want any more home games.*
- *Recognizing those who have fought in our away games. On September 10, Sgt. Maj. Thomas "Patrick" Payne, a Ranger assigned to the U.S. Army's Special Operations Command, received the U.S. military's highest honor for valor in combat—The Medal of Honor—for actions in rescuing 70 hos-*

*tages in northern Iraq in 2015. Also, Sergeant First Class Allyn Cashe, has recently been endorsed for the Medal of Honor for actions in Iraq from 2003.*
- *All those aforementioned continue to provide me with a renewed sense of resolve and resiliency as I have attempted to convey what Major General Tony Cucolo, (US Army, Retired) spoke of a few years ago to the graduating class here, when he challenged them to 'Live a life worth their sacrifice.'*

*In closing, students, I would like you to take away this:*

*We want to build and grow — and that's something essential about America. Those who attacked us had no respect for human life. We see dignity in every human being. That's part of what we value as Americans.*

*We go forward with confidence because we have something that our adversaries do not — we have a commitment to seek a future of justice, peace, and opportunity for those oppressed, all founded upon our Judeo-Christian principles.*

*When do we not think of the common sense in Thomas Paine's words, "These are the times that try men's souls?" For more than two centuries our nation has found its strength in the service of its citizens. Ordinary men and women who give of themselves for the common good.*

*Our legacy of service is now carried on by a new generation of Americans, who comprise less than 1% of the American population. Some stepped forward in a time of peace, not foreseeing years of combat. Others heed the words from Isaiah 6:8, "Then I heard the voice of the Lord saying, "Whom shall I send? Who will go for us?" "Here I am," I said; "send me." They have stepped forward in this time of war, knowing full well that they could be sent into harm's way.*

*Through their extraordinary service, our armed forces, and their families, have written a new chapter in the American story. And by any measure, they have earned their place among the greatest of generations.*

*I want to thank you for allowing me today to 'do my duty.'*

*May God and Saint John Paul II continue to bless our service members and their families, especially those currently deployed, those who have served, as well as the students, families, faculty, and alumni of Saint John Paul II Catholic High School, and may God continue to bless the United States of America.*

*Nolite Timere.*

*Support and Defend!*
*People First!*
*Army Strong!*

## Personal Reflection

- Below are oaths that I have taken on occasions when I was enlisted and when I became an officer, and had subsequent promotions:
- "I, _____, do solemnly swear (or affirm) that I will support and defend the Constitution of the United States against all enemies, foreign and domestic; that I will bear true faith and allegiance to the same; and that I will obey the orders of the President of the United States and the orders of the officers appointed over me, according to regulations and the Uniform Code of Military Justice. So help me God."
- "I, *[name]*, do solemnly swear (or affirm) that I will support and defend the Constitution of the United States and the Constitution of the State (Commonwealth, District, Territory) of ___ against all enemies, foreign and domestic; that I will bear true faith and allegiance to the same; that I take this obligation freely, without any mental reservations or purpose of evasion, and that I will well and faithfully discharge the duties of the Office of *[grade]* in the Army/Air National Guard of the State (Commonwealth, District, Territory) of ___ on which I am about to enter, so help me God."

## Contemplate

What oaths have you taken in your life? To whom do you swear that oath?

_____
_____
_____
_____
_____
_____

What do you consider the duties of citizenship?

_____
_____
_____
_____
_____
_____

How do you implement the duties of citizenship in your life? In others' lives?

_____
_____
_____
_____
_____
_____

# Discipleship

(1) One of the personal followers of Jesus Christ during his life, especially one of the Twelve. (2) One who follows or is influenced by the doctrine or example of another.

**Insight:** Matthew 4:19.

*He said to them, "Come after me, and I will make you fishers of men."*

Discipleship is certainly related to mentorship and membership in that we often find ourselves attracted to a particular person, but to that group or organization as well. There was a mixed lot of professions by those called by Christ to be disciples, each had a period of discernment; yet, once called, some still questioned why they were disciples. Following Jesus's death and resurrection, they had the mission to live out what Jesus had taught them.

I have previously stated that you have to be both a follower and a leader, as both are complementary to one another, and some consider them both sides of the same coin. Both followership and leadership are also part of discipleship.

**Inspire:** Having come from a family of nine siblings, I was granted the opportunity to observe discipleship in action from my parents and siblings. Although I have not always been the best son, brother, husband, (fill in the blank), there are certain aspects of discipleship I am able to absorb from my family.

**Ignite:** Acceptance.

*Burns family photo, 1967. Standing: Father, Mother, Patrick, Thomas, Catherine, Richard, Michael. Front row: Me, John, Timothy, Melanie.*

I have not only lost both parents, and a mother-in-law and father-in-law, but also have lost two of my brothers. My brother John died shortly upon return from Operation Iraqi Freedom (OIF) 06-08. He was # 5 out of 9 of us. In addition, my brother Tom, the oldest, and a postal worker, departed in 2015. Both were Disciples of Christ to the end.

This is another eulogy that I have given for our family. This specific eulogy was delivered for our brother John who passed away at age 50. I had recently returned from my first tour in Iraq in 2008. In addition to discipleship, there are the themes of God, family, and friends as well as the theme of humility and pride.

*　*　*

*I'm Francis, #8 out of 9 Burns children, John, # 5, was my older brother. We'll always be the nine. In the past 15 months, I have experienced plenty of loss with my military brothers-in-arms — both US and Iraqi ... now coming home we're confronted with the loss of one of my blood / fraternal brothers as I am transitioning coming back Stateside, trying to re-learn how to be a husband and father, now drawn here to be a brother and a son.*

*I immediately thought of my mom, the rock of our family, and a large part of the foundation of this parish. A quote from Mother Theresa came to mind: "I know God will not give me anything I can't handle. I just wish that He didn't trust me so much." When I arrived, she was on the phone saying the same to all as she did just over four years ago, but instead of stating that "We lost Tom" it changed to "We lost John." I'll attempt to find him and elicit some emotions to all gathered.*

*I believe that we all have something in common in that we feel that something is missing ... it certainly felt that way last night after the wake at 296.*

*Like most of you, I was unable to see him in the past couple of days. It is unknown to me what his last coherent thoughts were.*

*The last time I was up here, I was lamenting that my father did not get an opportunity to witness the Red Sox winning a World Series. John was fortunate enough to see them win a couple in the past few years, as well as a team called the Patriots do OK as well.*

*He had not been well the past 10 years or so. I ask that you not remember him in this way, or how he has been the past few years' health wise, which has certainly affected his physical and mental functions. It's almost as if we want to sing that Irish Rebel song, "Johnny We Hardly Knew Ya…"*

*On behalf of the US Postal Service, I would like to apologize upfront to everyone today who may not receive their mail today. As a testament to their affection to John, I think that all his co-workers are here, and I believe that they've essentially shut down operations for a bit the past few days. Guess stamps will go up again to make up for it.*

*He's always had God, Family, and Friends.*

*How do you remember him? John, Eggy, Johnny, Dad, Rooney, Burnsie, Whipper, John Joseph, Uncle John…*

*I've written some thoughts that have come to mind when I think about John…*

- *Watching him teaching Pat to walk by having him walk on his shoes as he held his arms*
- *Being with us on family vacations: Hampton Beach, U.S.S. Massachusetts, and Sturbridge Village.*
- *Getting a band to play on the basketball court for the "Back to School Party"*
- *Being an altar boy*
- *Working with Brian Brasili and Tim at Frank's Farm*
- *With Tim, waking us up to watch the US astronauts land on the moon on TV*
- *Washing his hair in the tub before school*
- *A little brotherly fighting with Tim; O.K. a lot, and many*

*yardsticks and furniture broken by Ma trying to separate them*
- *Bringing home an over-inflated football from St. Bernard's so we had one to toss around*
- *Hating to lose, especially in football with Leominster Dolphins and at St. Bernard's*
- *Basketball games on our court with his high school friends; and their road trips to Canada and other places — Puff, Ganutes, Boiton, Shaves, Skippy, Ant, Tuna*
- *Listening to the "Echoes of Erin" program on Sunday mornings*
- *A gift one Christmas from Tom and him: a catcher's mitt from Werner's fire sale*
- *Showing me how to shave*
- *Watching the "3" at "4"; to those not familiar, that's the 3 Stooges at 4 o'clock in the afternoon*
- *Teaching me to put cologne — British Sterling, English Leather — behind my ears before I went on a date*
- *How to lift weights, developing a program for me*
- *Talking to the Sentinel & Enterprise, to ensure that our football team received some positive ink*
- *Polishing my black high-top cleats and putting in new blue and gold laces before the Thanksgiving Day Football Games*
- *Like all my siblings, he looked out for me. Getting me a job at Victory Market, in the meat room, and ensuring I get the proper wage and hours*
- *Washing his new Firebird for me, and allowing me to take it to the Senior Prom*
- *Taking me to Irish Festivals across Worcester County, or remembering my ancestry, or teaching me the power of positive*

*drinking. I'll plead the 5th on what age I was when I had my first 5th*
- *Coming into our room in the cellar, and after having a couple or three beers, stepping on Danny Richard who was sleeping on the floor in our room*
- *John separating his shoulder when we were trying to throw him in the pool at the 4th of July party, and having to spend the whole summer with Pat and I, re-habbing the pool and taking us fishing. It truly was an Endless Summer*
- *Sense of humor—M-A-R G-I-E, M-O-U-S-E; setting up the mannequin in the cellar and leaving a light on for all to see*
- *Playing on the same men's softball team with him and two of my other brothers a few summers*
- *Being a husband and father*
- *Teaching me to be humble, but proud at the same time. This blend of humility and pride is perhaps one of his best traits that he passed on to his sons Brian and Garrett*
- *"Not on my shoes..."*
- *By example, sharing a love of writing and reading; writing his cartoon The Adventures of Butch and Dad*
- *Cathy and Mark taking him in at Thanksgiving because he didn't want to miss a day of work at the P.O. on the busiest day of the year*
- *Always the life of the party for many years—in Clinton, at his house in Leominster, at the Brasili's, or 296*
- *Willing, to a fault, for trying to assist others—almost as if his heart was too big*

I'll share what my youngest, Cavan, who is in 1st grade told me, as we were holding hands and walking together before I left, "Daaaaaaaaaaad, at schoooooool, we pray and say a decade of the rosary every day. Tomorrrrrrrrrrow, I'll ask my teacher to remember Uncle John, OK?" Last night when he called, he said they did say the rosary for him. Cormac stated that he too was very sorry, and if any of his brothers died, he would never be able to smile again. Guess I was pretty glum when I left.

His obit stated that he was a stellar football player at St. Bernard's, teams of which did not always come out in the correct side of the win-loss column but continued to grow and improve daily—perhaps an analogy with his life, in that he was actually never beaten, unfortunately he just ran out of time.

In closing, I remember returning from Basic Training over 25 years ago to be able to Hail John and Amy at their wedding. Here I am now saying Farewell after having returned again from some Army "Training," as he leaves us physically from this world to be in a better place with God. (I also used Catullus' Ave Atque Vale poem, as my tears were an offering to him. The poem is found on page 59.)

## Personal Reflection

- I am fortunate, grateful, and humbled to be a follower of Christ.
- With the losses I have experienced, I am reminded of E. Kubler Ross's book, *On Death and Dying*, and the five stages of death on which she wrote: Denial, Anger, Bargaining, Depression, and Acceptance. These stages are true with other losses in our lives.
- Again, it is clear to see that the...ships are not mutually exclusive. I find myself being triggered / enraptured by certain Bible verses and phases, or sometimes it may be a song, other times a certain smell, or an article of clothing, or a picture.

## Contemplate

What do you consider the characteristics of discipleship and why?
_____
_____
_____
_____
_____

Whose example (s) do you follow?
_____
_____
_____
_____
_____

What are the attributes in that person that makes you want to be a disciple of them?
_____
_____
_____
_____
_____

# Craftsmanship

An artisan who is skilled in clever or artistic work.

**Insight:** Exodus 31:3.

*"And I have filled him with a divine spirit of skill, and understanding, and knowledge, in every craft."*

WUKID, an acronym meaning, Wisdom, Understanding, Knowledge, Information and Data. Wisdom stems from understanding, which comes from knowledge, which comes from information, which comes from data. The critical link to each of these is the analysis, 'the why' or the interconnectedness of each. As with analysis, the spirit of God connects us in doing something well for its own sake.

**Inspire:** My father once told me, "I've got some work that needs to be done." My response was, "Oh yeah, how much will I make?" His response to me was, "To hell with you then." I then apologized. I recognized my mistake of placing the result on the external reward of being paid instead of performing a job to the best of my ability.

I can still recall the smell of kerosene in a musty cellar work-shop, while using calibrated stones and brushes to polish molds and dies, which would then be used to make some sort of plastic wear, be it a comb, sunglass frame, flatware, or pink flamingo. It was monotonous and tedious work; yet, once the plastic was injected into the molds, there was certain quality of the product it yielded. This may be similar to what is considered today to be an 'artisan'—be it in a distillery, brewery, roaster, crafts, clothing, and other goods.

**Ignite:** Example.

*An Army Retirement Ceremony.*

In David Brooks's book, *The Road to Character*, he discusses eulogy virtues or resume virtues.[71] As the thought implies, the résumé virtues are what one may use to receive an interview for a job, and for the most part are hard skills. Eulogy virtues are those which one would want to be remembered. We often focus on building careers instead of building character.

---

71. The Road to Character, David Brooks. Random House Trade Paperbacks. 2016.

Although veterans like to think that the military taught them resume virtues, they really learned eulogy virtues such as **Loyalty, Duty, Respect, Selfless Service, Honor, Integrity, Personal Courage,** and **Resilience.** And, although not in the Navy, we learned about…ships: relationships, hardships, leadership, friendship, mentorship, workmanship.

An example of use of eulogy virtue is found in the *Challenge of Command* by Robert Nye. The person writing this had in fact written his own eulogy, as he was the authority on his life. "I loved the Army: It reared me, it nurtured me, and it gave me the most satisfying years of my life. Thanks to it I have lived an entire lifetime in the 30+ years that I served. We all have but one death to spend, and insofar as it can have any meaning, it finds it in the service of comrades in arms. If there is nothing worth dying for— in this sense—there is nothing worth living for."[72]

One virtue that all Veterans possess in spades is humility, or what I like to call Vitamin H. They embrace discomfort. Whether it be going away when you're 18 (or younger in some cases), new State, new way of life, being in Germany 30 years ago for the Fall of the Wall, finding and marrying your wife, being at the Pentagon on 9/11, the Troop Surge in Iraq, or one of the last 126 left after withdrawal in Iraq (with no Security Agreement), or running an installation, they exhibit resiliency in action.

I have included two separate speeches that address craftsmanship in a different manner. In that there were many different Military Occupational Specialties (MOS), there were many different crafts that each retiree possessed.

This speech was given in July 2009 at a retirement ceremony

---

72. Challenge of Command, Roger Nye.

at Fort Polk, LA. I was probably more serious in this retirement speech as I was newly arrived at Fort Polk.

\*\*\*

*Distinguished guests, fellow commanders, Command Sergeants Major, soon-to-be-retirees, family, and friends.*

*Good Morning.*

*It is both an honor and a privilege to speak to you at this retirement ceremony as you move on to the next phase of your lives.*
  *Nonetheless, today, 29 JUU-LIGH, is a momentous time for you. Today is a date you'll always remember as it is the date you first joined the Army, or your Pay Entry Base Date (PEBD). For one, it is actually his second retirement. For a Chaplain it also commemorates the Chaplain Corps' birthday. It's also significant to retire in the year of the Non-Commissioned Officer. Today, we gather to honor you for your many years of dedication and selfless service to our country.*
  *Collectively, you have given over 250 years to our Army. That encompasses a good portion of the written history of America. All of you here are today's greatest generation.*
  *You have given of your time and lives. You have more than done your duty.*
  *Not only Soldiers — but also Family members — have earned our gratitude and respect. There have been separations, stress, combat, gaining new friends, keeping the old, but what a unique life it's been!!*
  *A round of applause for all of them, please.*

## Back Azimuths

*Service:*

*When I return home, parents, neighbors, aunts, and uncles, would often remark, "How are things in the service?" Maybe it was the same for you? After completing basic and advanced training or returning home from deployments, it seems that you were the one who had changed; yet, everything back at home seemed to be the same. Perhaps your training and experiences were now allowing you to see things from a different perspective. Were you constantly asking yourself, "What is my role? How does what I'm doing fit in to the big picture?"*

*I believe it boils down to Service. This word originates from the Latin word, servus, to put others first.*

*Think about the uniform that you wore: from pickle suit, Battle Dress Uniform (BDU), Army Combat Uniform (ACU) — and what was right over your heart. You in turn were not concerned about the last two letters ~~U.S. Army~~, your focus was on the U.S. ~~Army~~. It seemed it was always about someone other than you. Selfless service embodied your careers. Yet, finally, today is about you.*

*You, who have been through the Cold War when conflict was thought of more of a light switch which, if there was a conflict the switch was on, if not, it was off, to the current era of persistent conflict with the light switch always on, but more a dimmer switch in which the intensity waxes and wanes, but something is always going on. From Grenada, Panama, Desert Shield / Storm, Somalia, Kosovo, the Balkans, Operation Iraqi Freedom (OIF), Operation Enduring Freedom (OEF), you have learned throughout your years of service to maintain the balance, both at home and abroad, of the traits of being both a Samaritan and a Spartan.*

*The challenge for you has been to translate this into the*

*concept of a Good Samaritan and all the while being conscious of the need to be a Spartan at any moment.*

*Another analogy of the traits that you possess is to relate what Dave Grossman wrote in an article entitled,* On Sheep, Wolves, and Sheepdogs.

*If you have no capacity for violence then you are a healthy productive citizen, a sheep. If you have a capacity for violence and no empathy for your fellow citizens, then you have defined an aggressive sociopath, a wolf. But what if you have a capacity for violence, and a deep love for your fellow citizens? What do you have then? A sheepdog, a warrior, someone who is walking the hero's path. Someone who can walk into the heart of darkness, into the universal human phobia, and walk out unscathed. Here is how the sheep and the sheepdog think differently. The sheep pretend the wolf will never come, but the sheepdog lives for that day."*[73]

*The Soldiers retiring here today have consistently lived that day throughout their respective careers.*

*As you move on with your lives, your family will be happy that you will continue to have the same mindset as when you wore the uniform on Active Duty... which was not to feel exasperated or defeated or despondent because your days aren't packed with wise and moral actions. But to get back up when you fail and celebrate behaving like a human—however imperfectly—and fully embrace the pursuit upon which you have embarked.*

*In closing, hopefully I have captured some of what you have been through in your service to our nation and give those gathered here to honor you a small insight into what makes you tick.*

---

73. *On Sheep, Wolves, and Sheepdogs.* Dave Grossman. Retrieved December 23, 2008, from http://mwkworks.com/onsheepwolvesandsheepdogs.html.

*I think that by now you have figured out that the secret is that there is no secret. You recognized that if you were willing to do the work, even when you couldn't see the results immediately, you would be ultimately rewarded. Today is that reward for you. In closing, I believe that each of you have fought the good fight, have finished the course, and have kept the faith.*
    *Good Luck, God Speed, Remain Army Strong.*

\* \* \*

May 2011. Having been at Fort Polk for almost two years, I was coming towards the end of my tour there. I attempted to inject some humor into the ceremony; yet, still retain some thoughts on their years of service.

*Good morning all! HOO-AH! Thank you for coming this morning! In a bit, after the Soldiers and their loved ones are recognized, we'll be invited to sing "Old Soldiers Never Die, They Just Fade Away." But this is NOT a funeral; it's a Retirement Ceremony. But retirement ceremonies **are** like going to funerals—in a way. And as that famous baseball philosopher Yogi Berra says, (there will be several references to him in the first part of my words this morning), "We should always go to other people's funerals, otherwise they won't go to ours." So, this morning, I'll offer some thanks, lessons learned of the past 20+ years, and close with a Farewell to Arms (although it will not be the Hemingway novel).*
    *So, upfront, to all the retirees… "I want to thank you for making this day necessary." (Yogi'ism #2) Some of your co-workers and subordinates, as well as superiors have told me*

*that some cause happiness wherever they go; others, whenever they go. Which one are you? (#3)*

*For those who have spouses with them this morning, please forgive them for stretching that "for better or worse" part. (#4). Virtually every human emotion has been experienced by these Soldiers and their families, ranging from sheer joy to abject depression and everything in between.*

*To those families and friends who travelled here to Fort Polk, Welcome! In Louisiana, we're reminded that, "It ain't the heat, it's the humility." (#5) I was privy to some of the conversations in your cars while enroute here: "We're lost, but we're making great time!" (#6) Or, "I knew exactly where the ceremony was, I just couldn't find it." (#7) Thanks for being here to share in this day with your loved one,*

*From those with whom you have served throughout the years, they offer you their thanks for teaching them, mentoring them, humoring them, and sharing so many special and unique moments with them.*

*I trust that you will enjoy retirement, and again as Yogi (#8) reminds us, to take a two hour nap each day from 1 to 5. For spouses, think that is the for better or worse thing again.*

*So, 20+ years lessons learned:*
- *You have exhibited bravery in that bravery is being the only one who knows you're afraid.*
- *You have been convinced that to be happy means to be free and that to be free means to be brave.*
- *You have invariably been models of courage and fidelity.*
- *You have become self-aware, self-reflective, and self-critical.*
- *You have learned the value of being clear-eyed about yourself, "Don't deceive yourself, it is habit forming."*
- *You have experienced that the best two places for self-reflec-*

*tions are: battlefield or prison. I believe it was the former for all of you.*
- *You have reflected that time and distance can change and mature one's perspective.*
- *You have inculcated in your thoughts and actions not to bother to be better than your contemporaries or predecessors, but to try to be better than yourself.*

*You have truly lived and will continue to exemplify the words of Xenophon, in his book "The March of the 10,000" that "Those of us who recognize that death is a common and necessary portion of all humans, and therefore strive to meet death nobly, in common with others, with the hopes of thereby avoiding death, are precisely those who are able to reach a ripe old age and enjoy a happier existence while they do live."*
    *The following prayer found in Andersonville, Georgia, at the prisoner of war camp, after the Civil War. Author is unknown:*

*We asked for strength that we might achieve;*
*God made us weak that we might obey.*
*We asked for health that we might do great things;*
*He gave us infirmity that we might do better things.*
*We asked for riches that we might be happy;*
*We were given poverty that we might be wise.*
*We asked for power that we might have the praise of men;*
*We were given weakness that we might feel the need of God.*
*We asked for all things that we might enjoy life;*
*We were given life that we might enjoy all things.*
*We received nothing that we asked for*
*But all that we hoped for.*

*And our prayers were answered.*
*We were most blessed.* [74]


*Rear Admiral James Stockdale, Medal of Honor recipient from the Vietnam War, seven and half years Prisoner of War in North Vietnam, offered the following at a friend's retirement, "You have struggled through the winds, the sand, the rain, and the sleet; you have stared at the sun, and not been overwhelmed by it. Have a happy "rest of your life" and God Bless you."*
    *I pray that the coming years will be blessed with peace and prosperity for you, your families, and loved ones.*

*Army Strong.*
*Support and Defend.*
*All the Way!*

---

74. An Unknown Confederate Soldier. Retrieved December 23, 2008, https://www.goodreads.com/quotes/9235676-i-asked-for-strength-that-i-might-achieve-he-made.

## Personal Reflection

- You never know where your influence ends.
- Write a thank you note to a person who exhibits eulogy virtues. Tell them at least three things you admire about them.
- Things worth doing are worth doing well.

## Contemplate

Through the years, who has played a part in your development and why?

What do you think your eulogy virtues are?

What is the best way to pass along your eulogy virtues to others?

# Relationships
bring, carry back home.

*refero, referre, rettulli, relatus*, meaning "to be born or thrust in between things, taken substantively." [75]

**Insight:** James 1:19.

*"Know this, my dear brothers: everyone should be quick to hear, slow to speak, slow to wrath."*

This is called putting faith into action and is related to the understanding that no one is an island onto themselves. All that we do comes back into others. By listening to understand, you build trust.

**Inspire:** Build trust and develop relationships. That is a mantra by which I have tried to live. I believe that each of the aforementioned…ships hinges upon building trust and developing relationships.

---

75. *refero, referre, rettulli, relatus*. Retrieved February 2, 2022 from http://www.latin-dictionary.net/definition/33112/refero-referre-rettuli-relatus.

**Ignite:** Sometimes, it's OK to stare.

*Homer Winslow, Veteran in a New Field. The Alamo, San Antonio, Texas. Retirement Ceremony.*

This was written and delivered at The Alamo in May 2016. In a sense, it was the culmination of 30 years of Active Duty in the US Army. I call this my f-word speech, as its theme is Faith, Flag, Family, Friends, and Fun.

* * *

*No human being could fail to be deeply moved by such a tribute as this. Coming from a profession I have served so long and a people I have loved so well, it fills me with an emotion I cannot express."*[76]

— GEN Douglas Macarthur

*I have always wanted to say that…*

---

76. MacArthur, Duty, Honor, Country. American Rhetoric, Top 100 Speeches. Retrieved February 2, 2022 from https://www.americanrhetoric.com/speeches/douglasmacarthurthayeraward.html.

*So, the Master of Disaster, the Tower of Power, Too Sweet to be Sour, Every Man's Threat. He's on page #5 in your programs, but # 1 in your hearts... Sir, I thank you for those remarks and you and Margie being here today.*

*My brother Michael, not to be confused, with Mike Ferriter, thank you as well for the heartfelt remarks and recognition from Massachusetts—we'll always be the nine.*

*Also, upfront, JD and Sherri Driscoll—for the work done in here, as well as SGM Dougherty, the G3 Team, Public Affairs, and Protocol for ensuring that the event went off without a hitch.*

*And Blake Rubie, representing the 30,000 Installation Management Command (IMCOM) Department of the Army Civilian Workforce for singing the National Anthem, and Chaplain Giammona for the wonderful invocation.*

*Please join me in a round of applause for all those who made today special.*

*I will speak today about F-words*

*Since first name is Francis, known as Frank, Fran, and having only received one "F" in my life, and it was my Senior year in high school, 4th Quarter Calculus Final Exam 34 years ago, from Sr. Mary Clara, oh, I think that was actually a "D" but I digress...*

*This is NOT a Funeral, or is it about Failure, or Fear.*

*Or the word that begins with F and ends in UCK, yup, you know it—Firetruck*

*Rather, it is about the following F-words:*

*Faith | Flag | Family | Friends | Fun*

*All gathered today fit into one of the categories, some in a few, many in all.*

*Please allow me to shoot the proverbial back azimuth, or for those who have attended a Senior Service College or Fellowship, you can translate it to The Ends, Ways, and Means — now that I am at the End, it kind of explains the ways (methods that got me here) and the means (resources, mostly people and time investment) that got me here...*

*Let us begin with Faith — represents encouragement, and whose Latin root word is cors, cordis, feminine case, 3rd Declension, translated to "heart." (That's my obligatory Latin reference)*

"Life is a gift to me from my Creator. What I choose to do with my life is my gift back to Him."

— Billy Mills

*I have struggled, like all of us, to live up to that standard.*

*My faith and educational foundation were ingrained in me as a product of my twelve years of Catholic schooling and my devout Catholic parents for whom I am ever thankful. Thank you, Mom, for your gift of faith and your encouragement. The key to encouragement is in knowing what gives people courage — you continue to do so. Thank You. As Dad was fond of saying, "You done good."*

*John 15:13. "No greater love man has than this: to lay down one's life for his friends." Darlene had this inscribed on the Claddagh ring that she gave me a few years ago. More on what that means to me when I speak about the next F — Word...*

*Flag: Represents inspiration.*

*We wear it on our combat uniforms every day and everywhere, so, we do in fact wear our hearts on our sleeves. 3 flags have special meaning to me.*

*Many of you know that there's another Francis Bernard Burns, my father's brother, and my namesake. There is a folded American Flag on the wall in my office, and below it there is a Bronze Star with Valor and two Purple Hearts. Have been asked if that's mine, or my father's? Well, the background to the story is that in the Korean War, 13 years prior to the day that I was born, my namesake, Francis B. Burns, CPL, USMC, gave the ultimate sacrifice so that his Commanding Officer could be evacuated. Since his death day was my birthday, my parents decided to honor me with his full name. They thereby gave me a great opportunity, by giving me a great task: to live up to the honor of my valorous uncle.*

*Flag Ceremony: Those who have folded a flag, you may remember that there are 13 folds, and each has a different meaning, ranging from eternal life to womanhood to the valley of the shadow of death. The 13th and final fold, in the eyes of a Christian citizen, represents an emblem of eternity and glorifies, God the Father, the Son, and Holy Ghost. When completely folded, with the stars in the uppermost of the flag, and having the appearance of a cocked hat of our forefathers from the Revolutionary War, it reminds us of our national motto, "In God We Trust."*[77]

---

77. The meaning behind the 13 Folds of the United States Flag. Retrieved May 10, 2016 from https://nationalflagfoundation.org/the-meaning-behind-the-13-folds-of-the-united-states-flag/.

*"Midway along the journey of our life I woke to find myself in a dark wood, for I had wandered off from the straight path."*

— *Dante Alighieri*

*So, my midway along the journey of my Army life (and midway through this speech), was exactly 15 years in the Active Army, on 9/11, where I was in the Pentagon. Was able to experience terrorism first-hand, and all that that means, and then do my part not to have any more "Home" games, but to fight the "Away" games, and take the fight to the enemy. So, the other flag I always picture is the one that was draped over the side of the Pentagon.*

*Family: my motivation*
    *Darlene and the boys…*
*When you have a wife who has been a tower of strength and shown more courage than you dreamed existed—that's the finest I know. In the words of Johnny Cash, "Every time I look at you, I fall in love, all over again." Thank you, Darlene. I love you. (Present flowers)*
    *We have three Sons / or My 3 Sons (na-na na nah, na-na na nah…)—Conor, Cormac, and Cavan—living examples of Resiliency. Home for them is everywhere and nowhere at the same time. Late great, Merle Haggard, known as The Hag, summed up life as a military child when he wrote, "All my friends are gonna be strangers." Kind of makes sense to me now. We are extremely proud of the gentlemen that you have become.*
    *With inheriting Burns Family genetics of problematic heart, I have a very similar sentiment to Lou Gehrig's in that,*

*"I might have been given a bad break, but I've got an awful lot to live for."* With that, it truly is all about Family...

*Representing the Burns Clan, Go SOX!*

*Joined by my brother Mike from Fremont, CA along with his daughter Eileen and son-law Dale;*

*Rick, from Leominster, MA; Melanie from Wiscasset, ME*

*Brother Tim's wife, Ilsa, from Waco, TX, and their son Daniel, his wife Kim, and their son, Samuel from University of Dallas, just up the road a bit.*

*Brother Patrick and his wife Terry, from Shrewsbury, MA.*

*Thank you for your unwavering support throughout the years, and for being here this weekend.*

*The Archie Family from Naples, FL*

*Pop. The Senior USMC Representative, Veteran, Crew Chief, Korean War Vet, Made Staff Sergeant in two years.*

*Dave and Melannie, with their two sons, Colin & Quentin*

*And Doug's son, DJ.*

*Remember y'all when you demonstrated that "A fishing pole sinks faster than a tackle box."*[78]

*Thank all of you for travelling so far to be here and to share in this moment.*

*Other Family Members, "You Should Be Here..."*[79] *those who have been influential in my life and are no longer here with us — my Dad, Darlene's mom Peg, two of my brothers, John and Tom. All are certainly here in spirit, and I thank them as well.*

---

78. Three Year Old, Song by Eric Church. Retrieved December 10, 2021 from https://www.azlyrics.com/lyrics/ericchurch/threeyearold.html

79. You Should Be Here, Cole Swindoll. Retrieved December 10, 2021 from https://www.google.com/search?q=you+should+be+here+lyrics.

*Friends & co-workers:* As Tennyson wrote, "I am a part of all that I have met..."

Or a combination of Sir Isaac Newton & Michael Stipe — "Standing on the shoulders of Giants, leaves me cold..."

Appreciate folks travelling from CA, GA, AL, and DC. The things people do when they hear that there's free beer! They are more well-known more so by their nicknames, The 'Don,' Devo, Tall Paul, Catfish (also representing the Marine Corps). Knew you Fourteen Hundred and Fifty-Three Beers Ago, when "We Were Lieutenants Once, and Young" and were playing rugby (another F-Word, Fitness) in the then Federal Republic of Germany. I wish to thank every one of you — Thank you, thank you, thank you, thank you...

Although in the Army, today is also about... ships.

Specifically, Relationships and:

Leadership, Mentorship — Lieutenant General Ferriter and Margie Ferriter, Lieutenant General Dahl, Major General Patterson, Mr. Tindoll, Command Sergeant Major & Erica Hartless, thank you.

Workmanship, Craftsmanship — Commander's Initiative Group (CIG) folks Rhonda, Larry (from DC, go NATs!), Carol, and Marie (honorary CIGer), Central Region, Glenda and Command Sergeant Major Judkins, and all from the G3 Section. Also, from The Pentagon days in 2001, Pat Flynt, who to me, was the epitome of a professional. Thank you.

*Friendships:* Roger & Kim Shuck and Family and the aforementioned JD and Sherri Driscoll as well as Mark and Barb Bertolini from Fort Polk.

And the other friends, also known as co-workers — all part of the greatest team, The Army Team.

*Two quotes from Emerson come to mind when I think of Friends and Teammates:*

1. *"No member of a crew is praised for the rugged individuality of his rowing." Or*
2. *"It is one of the blessings of old friends that you can afford to be stupid with them."*

*Moving on...*

*Frequent Flyer: think logged in a few past couple of years. Wait, who put those F words in there...*

*OK, Fun.*

*Have tried to bring a little enjoyment to the office, work, or upon the fields of friendly or unfriendly strife.*

*Some days more so than others, as one of my Sergeants Major was fond of saying, "Life's hard, it's harder when you're stupid." No, he said, every day is not a 20-year day ... And with that, we have to at times, "Embrace the Suck," as well as the Mike Rowe (from Dirty Jobs) acronym SWEAT — Sweat and Work Ethic Aren't Taboo. Sometimes we have to drink water, take a knee and face out, and change our socks.*

*The funny thing is that they are exactly the same things that I learned and experienced as a young Lieutenant, and have it ingrained in me ever since — the importance of Patience, Fasting, Thinking, Listening; that Leadership and Followership are two sides of the same coin; and, never losing your sense of humor; yet, have the good sense of knowing when to use it.*

*Finale*

## Francis B. Burns

*"Out of old fields comes all new corn"*

*—Chaucer* [80]

*Look at the painting by Homer Winslow on your programs.*

*Right now, anyway, there is some parallel with where I'm going... or, as Yogi Berra was fond of saying, "The future ain't what it used to be."*

*As you can elicit from the painting, there are conflicting emotions with a Soldier's departure from wearing a uniform; yet it shows a former Soldier harvesting a field that once again yields the gift of golden wheat, which in Christianity is a symbol of salvation.*

*When someone asked me if I felt that I belonged to the Army, it was similar to Supreme Court Justice Antony Scalia when he was asked about being a Catholic and his thoughts on being a member of the Supreme Court and his ties to the Constitution. I responded that I belong to the Roman Catholic Church, I belonged to my Family, and I belong to the Constitution. The Army, is just one creature intended to preserve, protect, and defend the Constitution. The Constitution is the Army's creator. No creature can be greater than its Creator. I like the Army. I love the Constitution and have taken an oath to support and defend it.*

*Thank you for allowing be to indulge in some F-words (Faith, Flag, Family, Friends, Fun) today and how they have provided me a good, straight azimuth as well as providing the Ways and Means, as I worked towards the End the past couple two three decades.*

*I know you are expecting a Wizard of Oz Moment—Not*

---

80. The Parliament of Fowls, Geoffrey Chaucer. Retrieved December 10, 2021, from https://quotefancy.com/quote/1130646/Geoffrey-Chaucer-For-out-of-old-fields-as-men-saith-Cometh-all-this-new-corn-from-year-to.

*the, "Pay no attention to the man behind the curtain" quote; rather, when Dorothy is leaving Oz, she says, "Scarecrow, I'll miss you most of all."*

*I really can't narrow it down, so will have to say that, "To all those gathered here today, I'll miss you most of all."*

*Let us remember all those deployed, and in harm's way at home and abroad, who have put in their quantitative time or chronos that allows us to enjoy these qualitative or kairos moments.*

*As we move on from the hallowed grounds here at the Alamo, where others gave their all, let us remember the words of Galatians 6:10 and St. Francis of Assisi, that, "While we have time, let us do good."*

*My youngest would be all over me if I didn't say this, "Everybody Have Fun tonight, Everybody Wang Chung Tonight."*

*Thank You.*

## Personal Reflection

- All…ships are interdependent and built upon trust and developing relationships.
- By listening to understand, you build trust.
- I approached this Army retirement speech by shooting the proverbial back azimuth on my Active Duty Army career. I think that by writing this speech about so many of the…ships in my life, it gave me a spark to overcome what Stephen Pressfield referred to when he wrote about resistance.
- US Army Chief Warrant Officer Michael Durant in his book, In the Co*mpany of Heroes*, wrote that it's OK to look back, not to stare. Thank you for allowing me to stare a bit.

Back Azimuths

## Contemplate

Who do you need to listen more to in your life? At work?
_____
_____
_____
_____
_____

Whom have you recently thanked for their relationship to you?
_____
_____
_____
_____
_____

What is your favorite...ship and how is it connected to relationship?
_____
_____
_____
_____
_____

# Conclusion

I was influenced to start this collection by embracing the term: *Audentes fortuna juvat*—Fortune favors the bold. I first encountered this phrase at Fort Benning, Georgia. It was on a sign which was hung above the entrance to "Honor Hill," which was a small hill where US Army Infantry Soldiers culminated their final foot march prior to their graduation from One Station Unit Training. I have used this phrase in some emotional intelligence coaching and was reminded of the phrase while listening to a Tim Ferris podcast with Steven Pressfield.

Each of us has the capability and the capacity to develop these…ships. I encourage you to further develop each of these…ships and add more…ships to improve your life. Perhaps they are indeed the same ships that Longfellow referred, only now they are filled with insight, as well as what inspires, and ignites us.

# Acknowledgements

I believe that scars tell better stories than tattoos. If I had a tattoo, which I do not, it would be the above symbol.

Its meaning, from the bottom, working upwards:
- A Dash, which is the time in between one's date of birth and date of death
- A Circle with dot, which is a trail marker meaning "I'm coming home." This is also the grave marker for Lord Baden Powell, founder of Boy Scouts
- A Cross, as we all have our burdens to carry, as Christ did for all of us.

I believe the symbol I created stems from the above image of The Pope's Revenge, which I was fortunate to see when I visited Berlin (both east and West) with Darlene and Paul Devereaux in 1988. The legend is that there to be no crosses in communist East Germany, and the funds sent by the Pope were used to build a communications tower. After completion, it was noticed that no matter which way the sun shone, a cross was seen. Despite paints, chemicals, and replacing or glass by either re-concaving or convexing the glass, it still showed a cross.

With that, I would like to acknowledge and thank God for all that He has done and continues to do for us. Although the book is dedicated to my wife, all that I am, I owe to God.

I recently shared with someone that I was writing a book about back azimuths. Being former military, the person easily picked up on the compass analogy and past reflection. I was then asked, "How long did it take you to write it?" I smiled and thought of

---

81. https://wilkswroasting.com/2021/03/04/tv-tower/

the answer that Gen Mattis gave when he was questioned about making a decision based upon his experience. So, in a deadpan response, I stated, "About 30-plus years."

There are many, some who may not realize, that continue to have a positive and significant impact in my life. Although some have been written about in the previous pages, I would like to acknowledge a few more. I often use a line from Tennyson's Ulysses poem, "I am part of all that I have met." And so it goes …

My family. Darlene—the epitome of a Christian woman, your faith remains the trait that continues to cause me to love you. And our three sons—Conor, Cormac, and Cavan. I appreciate each of your commitment to serving others and am extremely proud of the gentlemen that you have become. I love all of you.

I, along with my eight other siblings, were afforded the opportunity to attend Catholic schools for 12 years by our parents, for whom I remain eternally grateful. I thank my immediate family for continuing to provide me a solid base and refuge in word and in deed. The Catholic education provided me a proper foundation upon which to build, as well as the desire to be a lifelong learner.

There are many of whom I have already written in this book who have kept me on the straight and narrow, and without whom capturing the different…ships would not be possible. A special thank you to those who provided a review of the manuscript. Your comments and endorsements were most welcoming and appreciated.

Thank you also to Deeds Publishing: Bob Babcock, his wife Jan, and Matt King, for the coaching and for ensuring the thoughts and emotions that I was trying to capture came through via many manuscript turns and edits. Your attention to detail and professionalism is exceptional.

To Brigadier Cheryl Kearney, who wrote an incredible Foreword to the book, and in turn brought out some things that were deeply moving to me. A couple of years ago, she had sent an encouraging note to me, and in the P.S. section wrote, "Write that book! I'll help you."

Bob Anderson, the ultimate encourager, who ensured that I write the book and emphasize both the emotional aspect and the Judeo-Christian principles throughout the book.

Also, thank the US Army for affording me the opportunity to develop and enrich the…ships.

Finally, thank you to the readers, who have shot the proverbial Back Azimuth with me.

# About the Author

Col. Burns has held a variety of leadership positions throughout his career, ranging from leading at the platoon level to an Army garrison. He has served both stateside and overseas, twice at the Pentagon, and has served for over thirty months on two combat tours in Iraq. He recently completed a City-County Management Senior Fellowship with the city of Austin. He currently serves as a Department of the Army Civilian at The Installation Management Command Headquarters, located on Joint Base San Antonio, Fort Sam Houston, Texas.

Col. Burns also served as Principal, Our Lady of Perpetual Help Catholic School in Selma, TX, where he led and ran the 501 c (3) non-profit school, and he is a certified Emotional Intelligence (EQ-i2.0) Practitioner.

Col. Burns holds Masters Degrees in Strategic Studies from the College of Naval Warfare and in Teaching from Fairleigh Dickinson University, and a Bachelor's Degree in Political Science from the University of Massachusetts at Amherst, with Minors in both Latin and Philosophy, and is a member of Eta Sigma Phi (National Honorary Society of Classical Studies).